ILLUSTRATED
ATLAS

For information about other World Book publications, visit our Web site
http://www.worldbook.com or call **1-800-WORLDBK (967-5325).** For information
about sales to schools and libraries, call **1-800-975-3250 (United States)** or
1-800-837-5365 (Canada).

2005 Revised printing

World Book, Inc.
233 N. Michigan Ave.
Chicago, IL 60601

Flags: © 2004 Dream Maker Software

The Library of Congress has cataloged a previous edition of this title as follows:

Library of Congress Cataloging-in-Publication Data

Illustrated atlas.—[Rev. ed.].
  p. cm.
 P. [4] of cover: World Book's illustrated atlas.
 Rev. ed. of: Illustrated atlas. 2000.
 Includes glossary, list of resources and index.
 Summary: Presents a brief history and key facts about each
country including its size, geographical features, wildlife, and
how its people live, work, and play.
 ISBN 0-7166-4038-4
 1. Children's atlases. 2. Geography. [1. Atlases.
 2. Geography.] I. World Book, Inc. II. Childcraft picture atlas.
Illustrated atlas. III. Title: World Book's illustrated atlas.
G1021.I3 2001
912—dc21   2001031000

ISBN 0-7166-4046-5

Printed in Singapore

6 7 8 9 10 11 09 08 07 06 05

ILLUSTRATED
ATLAS

World Book, Inc.
a Scott Fetzer company
Chicago

Flags: Some countries have a special state flag that only the government uses. It flies on public buildings within that country. Usually, a state flag is a national flag with a coat of arms added to it. When a country has a state flag, the national flag flown by individuals is known as a civil flag. Each country decides whether its civil or state flag will be flown at United Nations (UN) Headquarters. Generally, the flag that flies at the UN is the one used abroad for other purposes. The country flags that appear in this book are the ones that fly at the UN.

3423

ACKNOWLEDGEMENTS

The publisher gratefully acknowledges the following artists, photographers, publishers, agencies, and corporations for illustrations used in this volume. All illustrations are the exclusive property of the publisher unless names are marked with an asterisk*.

Illustrations

Introduction spreads: Valeria Petrone/Caroline Church (Maggie Mundy Illustrators' Agency) 8/9, 11, 14/15, 18/19, 22/23, 25, 32, 38/39, 40/41, 43; Peter Geissler (Specs Art Agency) 32, 42; Specs Art Agency 18, 22

Welcome spreads: Maggie Brand (Maggie Mundy Illustrators' Agency) 44/45, 60/61, 74/75, 88/89, 106/107, 118/119, 136/137, 154/155, 164/165, 182/183, 200/201, 218/219, 236/237, 248/249, 266/267

Countries spreads: Maggie Brand (Maggie Mundy Illustrators' Agency) 46/47, 62/63, 76, 90, 108, 120/121, 138/139, 166, 184, 203, 220, 238/239, 250/251

Animals and Plants & Animals spreads: Gabrielle Stoddart (Linden Artists Ltd) 28/29, 50/51, 66/67, 80/81, 96/97, 112/113, 126/127, 144/145, 158/159, 172/173, 190/191, 208/209, 226/227, 242/243, 256/257, 268; Mike Long, 50/51, 271

Plants spreads: Peter Geissler (Specs Art Agency) 26/27, 94/95, 124/125, 142/143, 170/171, 188/189, 206/207, 224/225, 254/255

Growing & Making spreads: Peter Geissler, Barbara Jones (Specs Art Agency) 52/53, 68/69, 82/83, 98/99, 114/115, 128/129, 146/147, 160/161, 174/175, 192/193, 210/211, 224/225, 228/229, 258/259

Peoples spreads: Steven Brayfield 195; Lynne Willey (John Martin and Artists Limited) 30, 54, 71, 85, 101, 117, 131, 148, 162, 176, 213, 230, 246, 261

Journey spreads: Maggie Brand (Maggie Mundy Illustrators' Agency) 58/59, 104/105, 134/135, 152/153, 180/181, 198/199, 216/217, 234/235, 264/265

Map symbols: Specs Art Agency; Mike Long

Pictograms: Richard Berridge

Maps

Map artwork: Tom MacArthur

Photographs

Alamy Images*
Aspect Picture Library*
Associates Press*
Australian High Commission*
Bill Bachman*
Blaine Harrington*
Bob & Ira Spring*
Bruce Coleman Collection*
Bryan & Cherry Alexander*
Corbis*
Corbis Stock Market*
D. C. Williamson*
© DPA from Photoreporters*
© Dorling Kindersley*
eStock Photo*
Fred Gebhart*
Geoslides Photographic Library*
Getty Images*
Isaac Hernandez, Mercury Press*
James Davis Travel Photography*
John Massey Stewart*
Panos Pictures*
Patricia Bahee*
Photo Researchers*
Picturepoint Limited*
Red Dot*
Sally & Richard Greenhill*
Susan Griggs Agency*
The Daily Telegraph Colour Library*
The Hutchison Library*
Tim Sharman, European Geographic Survey*
Travel Link*
TRIP Photo Library*
Trizec Properties*
Wolfgang Kaehler*
Zefa Picture Library*

CONTENTS

You and your world

Maps are drawings of our world. Some show all of the world, and others show parts of it. Maps show us what the world looks like, except that maps are flat.

Sally and her brother Tom are finding out about maps.

1 We are Sally and Tom. We live in Rome. This big city is the capital of Italy.

2 We are astronauts. Here's our spaceship. It's going to carry us high above the earth's surface. The spaceship has a window so we can look out.

Why don't you come with us?

There's the street where we live.

3 We're zooming higher. What a wonderful view! The houses look smaller and smaller as we speed upward.

4 Now we can see the city of Rome. Rome has many streets and parks. Our house now looks so tiny that we can hardly see it.

5 We're going faster and faster. We can't see our house any more but we can see nearly all of our country. There are many cities and towns down there. If we took a photograph now, it would be like a map of Italy.

From here we can see almost the whole country.

6 Now we can see the islands near our country. Can you see the blue water around them? Our country is one of a group of countries. Together they form a continent called Europe.

7 The rocket has carried us hundreds of miles (kilometers) into space. Now we can see the world—it's round, like a huge ball. But we can see only half the world. The other side is hidden from view.

There's our world!

9

Globes and maps

Round maps of our world are called globes. The surface of the globe is printed with information that shows the world's land areas and seas. Globes are often mounted on stands so that they can turn. When you slowly turn a globe, it's a bit like traveling in a spaceship around and around the earth.

Maps show us many things about the land. A map of your town can show you where your school is or where to find the library. A map of the world will show you where all the many countries are. Because we can't fly up in a spaceship like Tom and Sally, we can't see the land from above. But maps can give us much of the information we need.

A globe is a round map of our world.

This photograph shows the outline of Italy and some other countries in Europe. If Sally and Tom took a photograph of Europe from their spaceship, it would look like this. Part of the land is hidden by white clouds.

A map of part of Europe shows us the same area that Tom sees from the window of his spaceship. But the map shows other things too. It shows the names of some of the countries in Western Europe and the names of some of the largest cities. This map gives us more information than a photograph taken from the spaceship.

A book full of flat maps is called an atlas. You can find a lot of information about all the countries of the world in an atlas.

Are you going on a vacation to another country? Turn a globe and find out exactly where that country is. Does it look far away from your country?

Do you have friends or relatives in another country? You could use a globe or maps to find out more about that country.

If you could take a globe and peel away the surface, it might look like this. A world map is like the surface of a globe laid out flat.

Our world

The world is round, like a huge ball. This world map is a flattened picture of the surface of the earth.

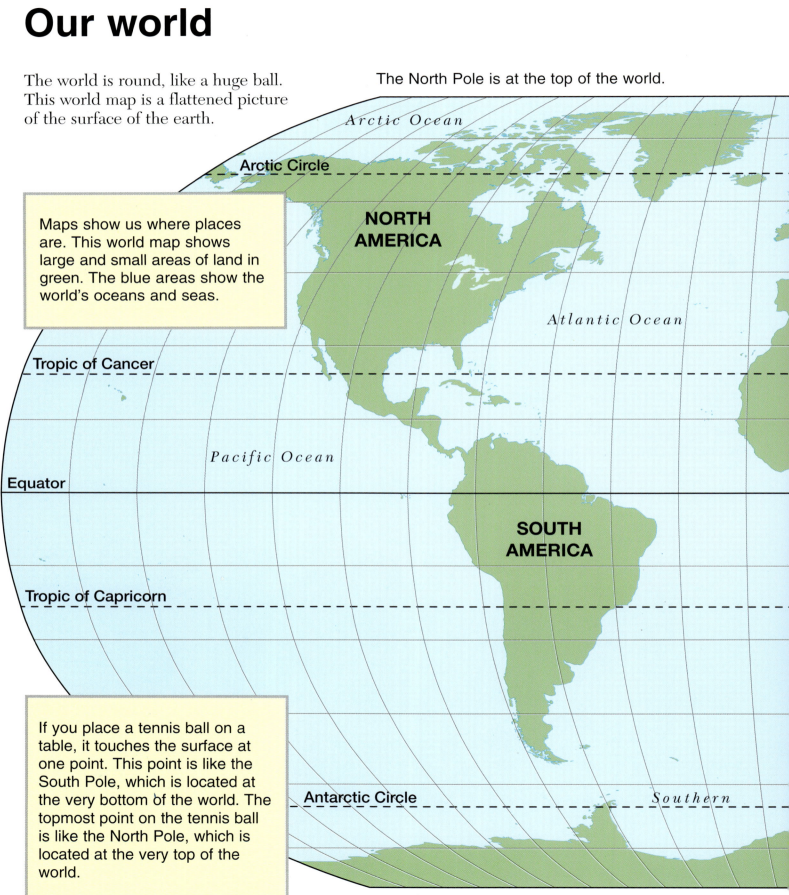

The North Pole is at the top of the world.

Arctic Ocean

Arctic Circle

NORTH AMERICA

Atlantic Ocean

Maps show us where places are. This world map shows large and small areas of land in green. The blue areas show the world's oceans and seas.

Tropic of Cancer

Pacific Ocean

Equator

SOUTH AMERICA

Tropic of Capricorn

If you place a tennis ball on a table, it touches the surface at one point. This point is like the South Pole, which is located at the very bottom of the world. The topmost point on the tennis ball is like the North Pole, which is located at the very top of the world.

Antarctic Circle

Southern

The South Pole is at the bottom of the world.

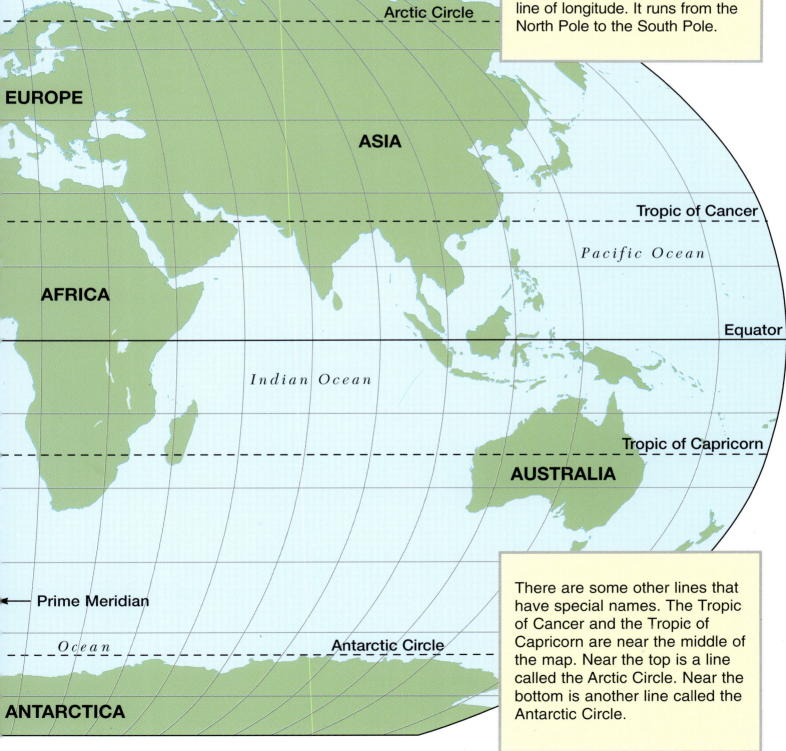

There are many imaginary lines on this map. They help people find exact places. The lines are called lines of latitude and longitude. The equator is a line of latitude that goes all the way around the world. It lies exactly halfway between the North and the South poles. The Prime Meridian is a line of longitude. It runs from the North Pole to the South Pole.

Arctic Circle

EUROPE

ASIA

Tropic of Cancer

Pacific Ocean

AFRICA

Equator

Indian Ocean

Tropic of Capricorn

AUSTRALIA

Prime Meridian

Ocean

Antarctic Circle

ANTARCTICA

There are some other lines that have special names. The Tropic of Cancer and the Tropic of Capricorn are near the middle of the map. Near the top is a line called the Arctic Circle. Near the bottom is another line called the Antarctic Circle.

The continents

Land covers about one-third of the surface of our world. The rest is water. This land is made up of seven main areas. Each of these areas is called a continent. Each continent also includes some islands.

The largest of the seven continents is Asia. The second largest is Africa. North America comes third and South America fourth. Antarctica, the fifth largest continent, surrounds the South Pole at the bottom of the world map. Europe is the sixth largest continent and Australia is the smallest.

Only about one-third of the earth's surface is covered by land. And most of this land lies above the equator. Water covers most of the earth below the equator.

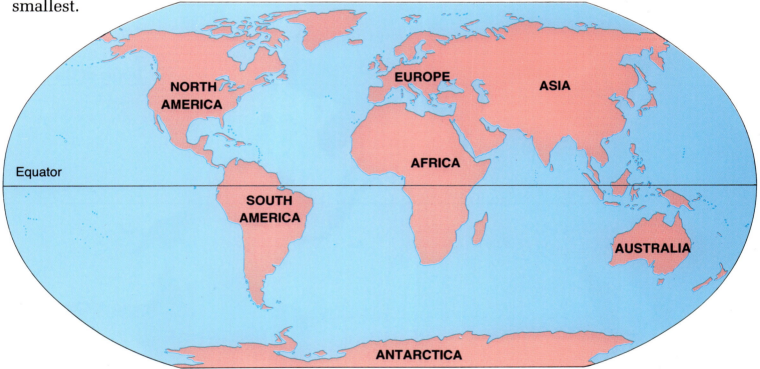

Water surrounds some continents. Others are joined. The imaginary line between two continents is called a border. For example, North America is joined to South America by a narrow land border. The border between Europe and Asia stretches many thousands of miles (kilometers).

Look carefully at the world map and you will see that each continent has its own special shape. At first glance, you might think that South America and Africa look similar. Both are wide at the top and narrow at the bottom. But look again. You will see that South America tapers almost to a point, like a carrot. The bottom of Africa is much wider.

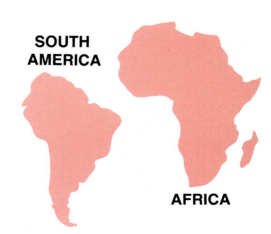

14

Here are four shapes.
Which one is Australia?

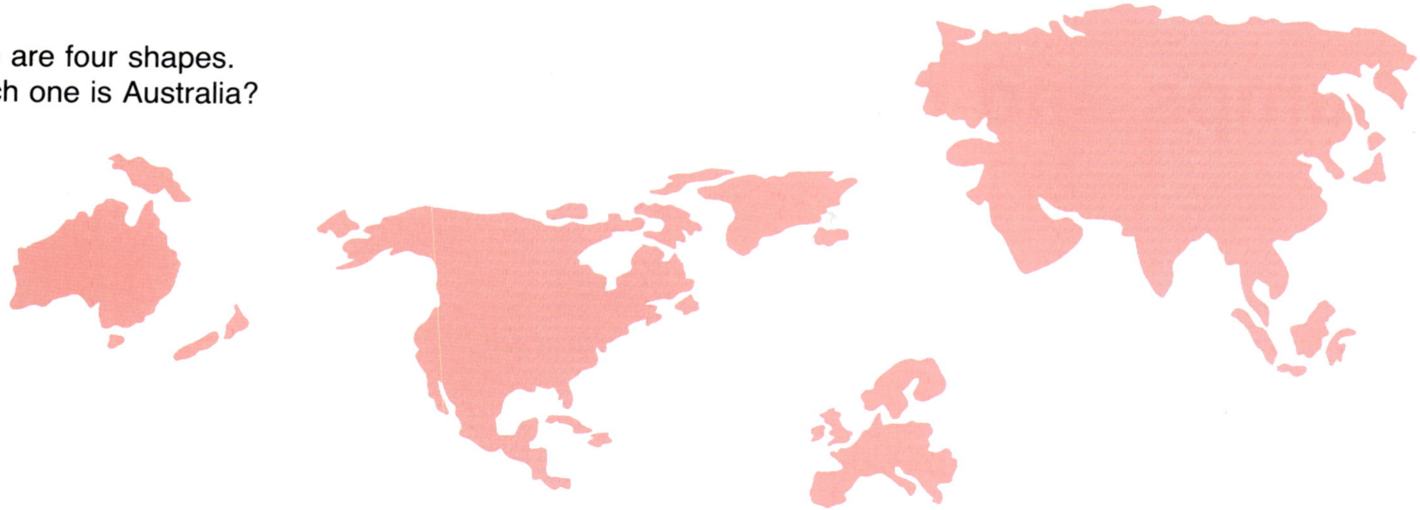

*Some maps are
drawn to scale.
This is what
it means.*

Scale on a map

Most maps are drawn to
scale. This means that a
certain distance on a map
stands for a certain distance
on the ground.

The straight line of the
equator across Sally's map
stands for the length of the
equator around the earth.
This length is about 24,902
miles (40,076 km).

   Sally measures the length
of the equator on her map. It
is 12 inches (30.5 cm) long.
This means that one inch (2.5
cm) on this map represents
about 2,000 miles (3,200 km)
on the earth.

Bumps and dips

The surface of the land is not flat all over. There are many parts that dip down and many that reach up high. Flat areas of land are called plains. The smaller bumps are hills and the larger ones are mountains. The dips are valleys. Sometimes the valleys are filled with water. Large stretches of water that gather in wide valleys are called lakes. Other valleys have rivers flowing through them, carrying water from the land to the sea.

Plains, mountains, lakes, and rivers can be shown on maps. They are shown as simple drawings called symbols. The symbol for a river is usually a blue line. Every time you see a blue line on a map in this book, you will know that a river runs through that part of the land. Here are some of the symbols you will see in this book.

When it rains, some rain water flows over the ground into **rivers.** The rivers slowly wear away rocks as they flow over them, making some of the world's valleys. Finally, the rivers flow into the sea.

mountain

lake

river

plain

Mountains are high areas. Many are capped by snow. Sometimes mountains occur in long lines called ranges. Most mountain ranges have been squeezed up by great pressure inside the earth.

Lakes form in dips in the land. Many lakes are filled by rivers that flow into them.

Plains are wide, flat stretches of land. They are found at both high and low levels, along the coast and farther inland, too. High plains are called tablelands, or plateaus.

Our watery world

On the world map, you can see that water covers more than two-thirds of our world. Imagine you were an alien in a spaceship! When you first caught sight of the earth you would probably name it "The Watery Planet."

The world's water is divided into large areas called oceans. The biggest ocean is the Pacific Ocean. It separates North and South America from Asia and Australia. It is so big that all the continents could fit into it. The second biggest ocean is the Atlantic. The third largest ocean is called the Indian Ocean. The fourth biggest ocean is the Southern Ocean. It surrounds the continent of Antarctica at the bottom of the world. The fifth largest ocean is the icy Arctic Ocean around the North Pole.

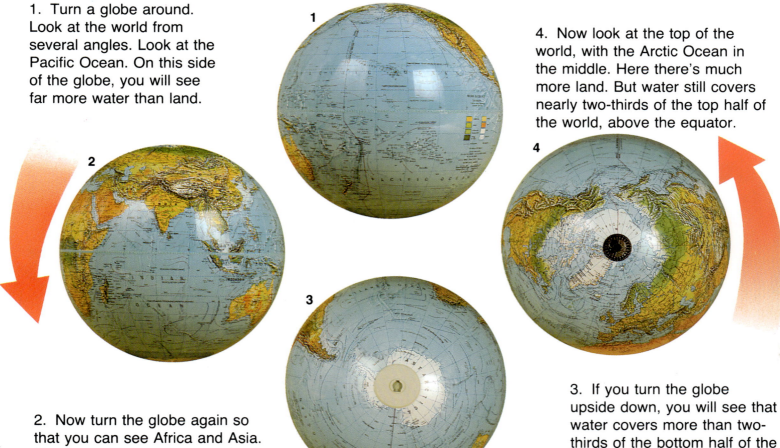

1. Turn a globe around. Look at the world from several angles. Look at the Pacific Ocean. On this side of the globe, you will see far more water than land.

4. Now look at the top of the world, with the Arctic Ocean in the middle. Here there's much more land. But water still covers nearly two-thirds of the top half of the world, above the equator.

2. Now turn the globe again so that you can see Africa and Asia. Now you will see a lot more land. But there's plenty of water.

3. If you turn the globe upside down, you will see that water covers more than two-thirds of the bottom half of the world, below the equator.

The waters of the oceans mix together. They are all part of one world ocean. You can see this on the map. The dividing lines, or borders, between oceans are shown in red. For example, the border between the Pacific and Atlantic oceans is an imaginary line running down from the tip of South America. Can you see the other ocean borders?

Oceans cover big areas. Each ocean contains smaller areas called seas. Seas are partly surrounded by land. Gulfs are large inlets of the oceans. Bays are smaller inlets. Straits are narrow strips of water that link larger parts of the oceans.

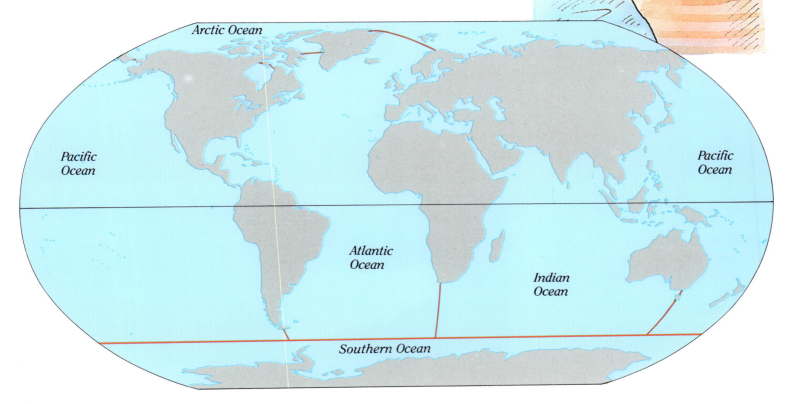

These two maps show some bays, gulfs, straits, and oceans. Can you find the Bay of Biscay, the Gulf of Mexico, the Strait of Gibraltar, and the Mediterranean Sea?

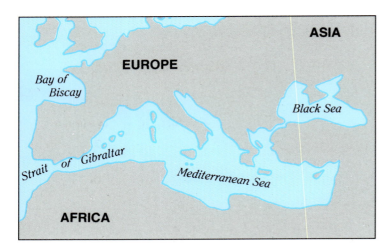

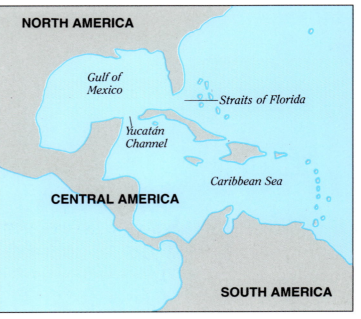

Ocean bumps and dips

The land isn't flat under the sea.

From the edge of the shore, the continents slope down to the lowest parts of the oceans. If we could pump out all the seawater, we would find some large flat plains on the ocean floor, but we would also see bumps and dips—just as on land.

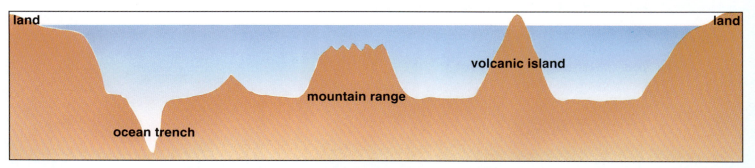

land | land

volcanic island

mountain range

ocean trench

Long mountain ranges, bigger than any on land, rise from the ocean floor. Some of these are so high that their tops rise above the waves. The tops form **islands.**

The deepest dips in the oceans are long valleys called trenches.

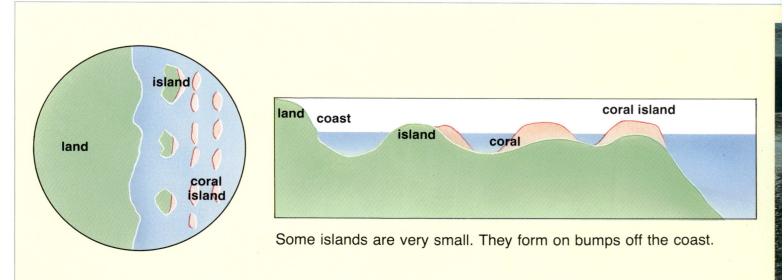

island

land

coral island

land coast

island

coral

coral island

Some islands are very small. They form on bumps off the coast.

Many islands in the middle of the oceans are the tops of volcanoes. The volcano starts to build up on the ocean floor. Hot liquid rock, or lava, is thrown out from inside the earth. The lava hardens in the water and piles up layer by layer. When the layers rise above the surface, an island is formed.

coast

island

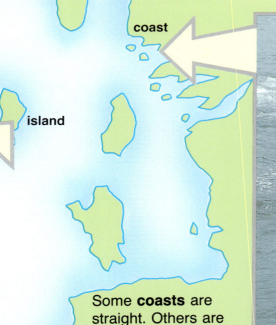

Some **coasts** are straight. Others are jagged and have deep sea inlets.

The oceans contain many low coral islands. Coral is a hard substance. It is made by tiny sea animals called coral polyps. The polyps live in large groups and produce thick layers of coral. Coral islands form on the tops of underwater volcanoes and along coasts. Coral islands have formed on bumps off the coast of northeastern Australia. This is the Great Barrier Reef, the world's biggest bank of coral.

21

Hot places, cold places

The sun gives our world light and heat. The heat is strongest around the middle of the world. This means that lands near the equator and the two tropics are hot most of the time. The sun's heat is much less strong near the North and South poles, where it is cold for most of the year. This is partly because the sun's rays are spread over a much larger area.

Places that lie between the poles and the tropics have much more changeable weather. These places usually have four seasons—winter, spring, summer, and autumn. Summers are warm, but not as hot as places near the equator. Winters are cold, but not as icy as near the poles. These large areas, called zones, are known as *temperate zones*. Temperate means neither very hot nor very cold.

Not all places in the world fit into this pattern of hot and cold. You can sometimes find snow on the equator. Very high places, like mountain peaks, are much colder than low places. For this reason, high mountains can be cold and snow-capped even when they are in the hottest parts of the world.

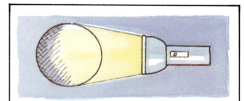

Shine a light at a ball. You will see that the most brightly lit part of the ball is the middle. The top and bottom parts of the ball get less light. In the same way, the middle parts of the earth get more light and heat from the sun than places near the poles.

This map shows how the zones of the world become colder the farther away they are from the hot, middle parts of the world.

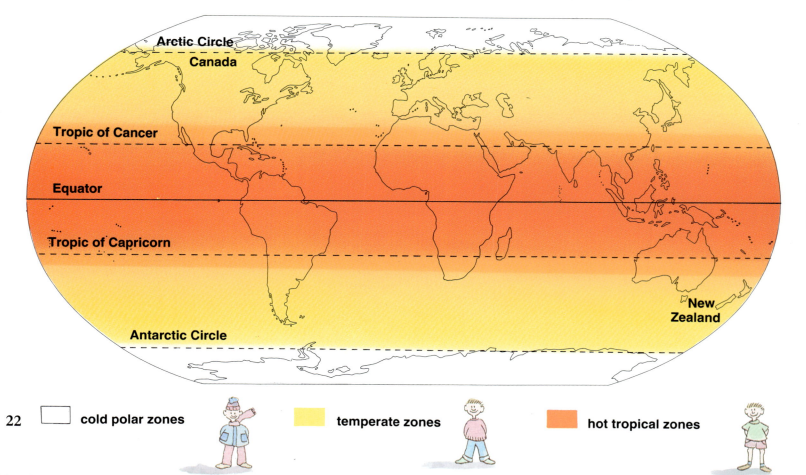

Arctic Circle

Canada

Tropic of Cancer

Equator

Tropic of Capricorn

Antarctic Circle

New Zealand

cold polar zones   temperate zones   hot tropical zones

The world's axis is an imaginary line that runs right through the center of the earth from the North Pole to the South Pole. This imaginary line isn't upright like a flagpole; it is tilted because the world leans on its side.

As the earth travels around the sun, first the top half and then the bottom half of the world leans toward the sun. When the top half leans toward the sun, it gets more heat than the bottom half. This means that when it is summer in a country in the top half of the world, such as Canada, it is winter in New Zealand in the bottom half.

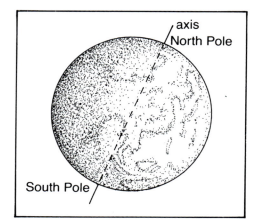

All the seasons are reversed between the top and bottom halves of the world.

summer in Canada

winter in Canada

winter in New Zealand

summer in New Zealand

23

Wet places, dry places

When people talk about the weather, they talk about the temperature—that is, how cold or hot it is. They also talk about rain. Some places have rain almost every day. Other places do not get a single drop for several years. Cold places get snow instead of rain. The kind of weather a place gets over a long period of time is called its climate.

Our world can be divided into regions that share the same kind of climate. For example, regions near the equator are hot, but they usually get plenty of rain. However, near the Tropics of Cancer and Capricorn, there are hot deserts that get hardly any rain. Between these deserts and the icy polar regions are the temperate zones. Some temperate zones are rainy, and others are dry.

■ Rainy

■ Dry

■ Cold

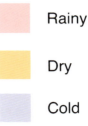

Equator

The coldest and some of the windiest places in the world are located around the poles. During storms called blizzards, strong winds drive snow across the land.

Some polar lands are always covered by snow and ice. In other areas, called the tundra, the snow melts during a short summer.

Deserts have few plants. Parts of some deserts have had no rain for hundreds of years. Many deserts are hot year-round. Other deserts have extremely cold winters.

Regions near the equator are hot. The temperature never falls below 80° F. (26° C) in most places during the day. Some places have rain every month of the year. Other places have a wet season and a dry season. The rainiest regions are often covered by forests. Drier areas are covered by grasses.

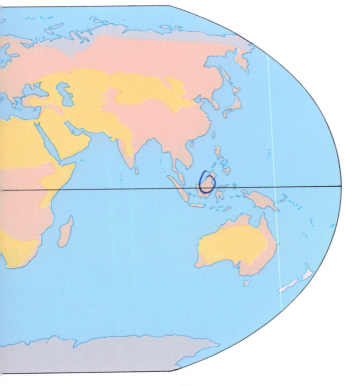

World records

Highest recorded air temperature
AL-Aziziyah, Libya, 136° F. (58° C).

Lowest recorded air temperature
Vostok Station, Antarctica, – 129° F. (– 89° C).

Wettest place
Mount Waialeale, on the island of Kauai in Hawaii, has an average annual rainfall of 460 inches (1,168 cm).

Sunniest place
Eastern Sahara, southern Egypt, over 4,300 hours of sunshine per year!

Driest place
Arica, Chile, where the average annual rainfall was 3/100 inch (0.76 millimeter) for a 59-year period.

Record wind speed
Mount Washington, New Hampshire—a speed of 231 miles (372 km) per hour.

Plants of the world

You won't find a cactus at the South Pole. Our world is covered with plants, but if you travel from place to place, you won't find exactly the same plants everywhere. Some grow better than others in certain places.

Some of the most important plant regions are shown on this map. The pictures on the map are symbols. They show the kinds of plants found in each of the regions. Watch for the special symbols on the **Plants** pages of this book. Some of the plants shown have no common names in English. In those cases, only the scientific names are given.

In the cold tundra regions, where the snow melts for part of the year, small plants and shrubs grow. But it is too cold and windy for trees. No plants grow in places that are always covered by ice.

 The hot, steamy rain forests near the equator contain the most types of plants. These include tall, upright trees, such as mahoganies and rosewoods, together with vines, orchids, and ferns. The largest of these forests are in South America and Africa.

You will find six different colors on the maps in this book. Each color stands for a kind of climate.

Look for all these colors on the map:

| tropical | high | dry | temperate | cold forest | polar |

In the cold forests, trees like firs, pines, and spruces grow. They are mostly conifers, which are trees that grow cones and have thick bark to protect them against the cold.

In warm temperate regions, many trees, such as maples and oaks, shed their leaves in autumn.

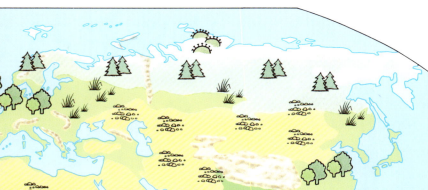

Grasslands can be found in regions that are too dry for many trees. The prairies of North America and the steppes of Europe and Asia are dry grasslands. Other grasslands can be found in the hot regions of the world near the equator, where there is a long dry season.

The plants found in deserts must live without rain for long periods of time. Some, like cacti, have thick stems that store water. Some deserts have few plants. They are covered by sand or rock.

Animals of the world

Animals live everywhere—in the hot deserts, in the icy polar regions, in the deep oceans, and on steep mountain slopes. Many animals could not live in any other region but their own. For food, they depend on the plants and other animals that share their region, and they become used to the climate.

Some animals find it hard to survive the conditions of a place all year. Some survive a cold winter by hibernating—going to sleep in a sheltered place. Others migrate, or move for part of the year to a region that suits them better. Many animals have changed, or adapted, to live in certain places. But it has taken them tens of thousands of years to do so.

The **Animals** pages of this book tell you about some of the world's wild animals and their homes, or habitats. The maps show you in general where some of the wild animals in each region live. Many of these animals can be found in other regions, too.

monkey

snake

chimpanzee

Polar bears live around the Arctic Ocean. Their thick, oily coats keep them warm. And their furry feet help them run swiftly over the ice. Like polar bears, most animals have bodies especially designed to help them survive.

polar bear

Most rain forest animals, including snakes, birds, and insects, live in trees where they can find plenty of food. Other tree-living animals are monkeys and chimpanzees in Africa, and orangutans and gibbons in Southeast Asia.

giraffe

wildebeest

elephant

Grasslands are home to many large, plant-eating animals, such as the elephants and giraffes of Africa. In the dry season, most of these animals migrate across the vast grassy plains in search of water and fresh plants to eat.

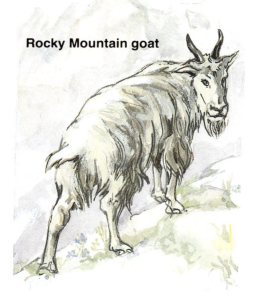

Rocky Mountain goat

arctic tern

reindeer

Mountain animals must be sure-footed, because they have to climb steep slopes. The Rocky Mountain goat is one of the finest animal mountaineers. Under its coat of white hair is a warm, woolly undercoat.

Animals that spend all their lives in polar regions must be able to keep warm. Some, including reindeer and many birds, spend the summer in the polar regions but migrate to warmer places when winter begins.

camel

koala

Desert animals must cope with great heat and thirst. Camels can go for long periods without drinking or eating. Their humps, which are made of fat, are like built-in supplies of food.

Some animals eat only a very few kinds of foods. For example, the leaves of the eucalyptus, or gum tree, are the main food of the koalas of Australia. Without these trees, the koalas might starve.

29

People of the world

There are billions of people living in the world today. And all of them are related to each other. All people belong to the human race.

But all people don't look or talk or spend their free time in exactly the same way. These differences depend partly on where they live. People change, or adapt, to suit the place around them.

People have learned to eat the food that grows best in their region. Rice, for example, grows well in hot, wet regions. It has been grown in Asian countries for many hundreds of years, and it is still the main food of people living in those parts. Wheat is more important to the people of Europe, Russia, and North America. These people use wheat to make bread.

These are just some of the people you will find in this book. Sometimes people are shown in their traditional dress.

People usually wear the kinds of clothes that are most suitable for their country's climate. The Inuit of northern Canada wear thick, padded clothes to protect them against icy winds. In North Africa, many people wear loose, flowing robes to keep them cool in the heat.

All over the world, people live their lives in different ways. They speak many languages, grow up in different kinds of homes, and go to many types of schools. And, because people have moved from place to place to mix and live with each other, there can be many different kinds of peoples living in any one region. In this book you will find out about the everyday lives of people all around the world.

People living in cold regions need to wear thick clothes to keep them warm.

People living in very hot regions wear loose, light-colored clothes to keep them cool.

Looking after the people

Many children will never get a chance to look at a book like the one you are reading now. And some will go through their lives without learning to read at all. For some people, life today means being safe, comfortable, and well fed. For others it means living in overcrowded, unclean conditions and never having enough to eat.

The rich countries of Europe and North America help the poor or "developing" lands in parts of Africa, Asia, and South America. They help by providing money, education, and training. But the changes are slow to happen, and there is much work to be done before everyone can have a good quality of life.

31

Your country, my country

Where does your country end? Many countries have sea-coasts, so the seas are the edge of those countries. Other countries lie side by side. The places where these countries meet are called borders. Some borders, like mountain ranges and rivers, are natural features. People mark out other borders with walls or fences. Some borders are not marked. People can cross freely from one country to another.

In many countries, the people speak the same language. They feel proud of their history and way of life. Sometimes the people of two countries fight each other. The winner may take some land from its neighbor. So, after a war, the border between the two countries may be changed.

Using a passport

When you visit another country, you usually need to have a passport to show who you are and where you are from. When you enter the country, immigration officers may ask how long you plan to stay and check what you are carrying before they let you stay for your visit.

Rivers form natural borders. They are easier to cross than high mountain ranges. The Mekong River in Southeast Asia forms the border between two countries—Thailand and Laos. Lakes also form borders in some places.

Mountains are natural borders. In the past, crossing them was difficult and dangerous. The people on one side of a mountain range often knew nothing about the people on the other side. Today there are good roads and often tunnels through which people can travel. The border between France and Italy runs through high mountains called the Alps. Roads and tunnels cross these mountains, connecting the two countries.

From 1961 until 1989, a wall cut the German city of Berlin in two. On one side of the wall was East Berlin, a part of East Germany. On the other side was West Berlin, a part of West Germany. But in 1989, this man-made border was torn down. And in October 1990, East Germany and West Germany were reunited into a single country. 33

Using our land

Every country has things of value, such as rich soil or a good supply of water to grow crops, or fuels that can be dug from the ground. These are called natural resources. Other important resources include trees, from which comes the wood to make furniture and paper, and ores from which people get metals.

The kinds of crops that can be grown in any place depend on the climate. Wheat grows well in temperate regions with warm summers, but rice needs hotter and wetter conditions. Rice is often grown on flat areas like steps, cut out from the earth. These are called terraces. The world's main food crops are wheat, rice, corn, and potatoes.

In places that are too dry for growing crops, farmers often graze cattle, sheep, or goats. Cattle are very important farm animals. They are raised for their meat, dairy products, and skins that are used to make leather. Sheep are raised for their wool as well as for meat.

UNITED STATES
OF AMERICA

This is the symbol for wheat. Wheat is the most important food crop in temperate countries. It is used to make flour. The world's top wheat producer is China.

34

This world map shows only the top producers of several important crops and farm products. These things are produced in many other countries, too. Each has its own symbol. Watch for other symbols like these on the **Growing and making** pages of this book.

🌽	corn	🌾	rice
🫗	dairy products	🌱	cotton
🐄	cattle	🧊	sugar
🥬	vegetables	🐑	sheep
🌾	wheat		

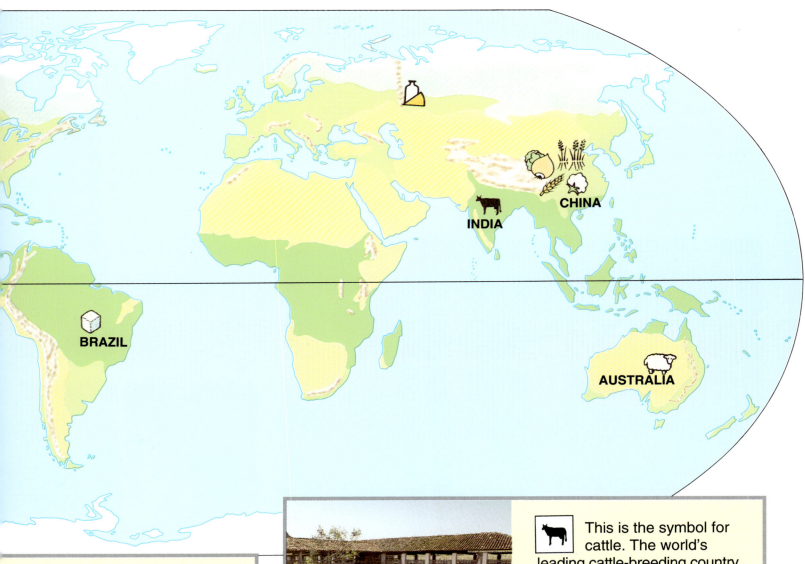

CHINA

INDIA

BRAZIL

AUSTRALIA

🌾 This is the symbol for rice. Rice is the chief food of about half the world's people. It is the most important food in Asia. The world's leading producer is China.

🐄 This is the symbol for cattle. The world's leading cattle-breeding country is India, where cattle are kept mainly for milk and for plowing. There are large cattle ranches in Brazil. Russia and its neighbors produce a lot of butter.

Treasures from the earth

There are hidden treasures of all kinds under the ground. Three of these treasures are coal, oil, and natural gas. These are fuels used to heat houses and to make electricity. Gasoline, which is made from oil, is used to run cars.

Rare stones, such as diamonds, and precious metals, such as gold and silver, are found in the rocks in some parts of the world. They are used to make jewelry, and they also have many uses in industry. One very important mineral found in the ground is bauxite, which is used to make the metal aluminum. Metals such as iron, from which steel is made, and copper, tin, and zinc are found in some rocks. Factories use minerals and metals from the ground to make many useful things.

Digging minerals from the ground is called mining. Some mines are holes dug into the surface of the land. Other mines are sunk deep down under the earth.

This is the symbol for coal. Here, a miner is digging coal from a mine deep underground. Coal is found in many parts of the world. China produces more coal than any other country.

This world map shows only the top producers of several important fuels and minerals. These minerals and fuels are found in many other countries, too. Each has its own symbol. Watch for other symbols like these on the **Growing and making** pages of this book.

coal

oil

gold

copper

diamonds

iron ore

bauxite

tin

natural gas

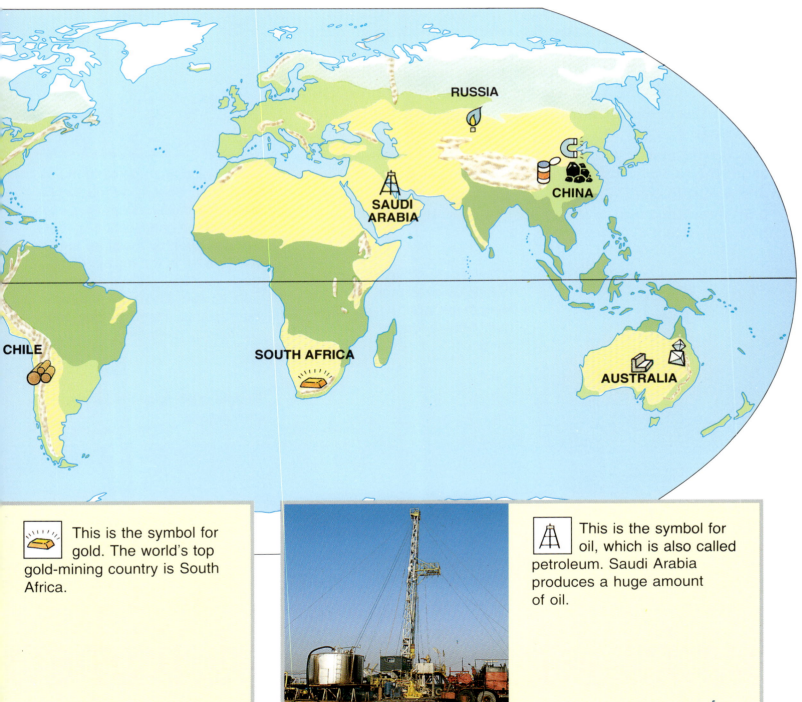

RUSSIA

SAUDI ARABIA

CHINA

CHILE

SOUTH AFRICA

AUSTRALIA

This is the symbol for gold. The world's top gold-mining country is South Africa.

This is the symbol for oil, which is also called petroleum. Saudi Arabia produces a huge amount of oil.

Taking care of our world

People are changing the world. If all the changes were good, our planet would always be a wonderful place on which to live. But, sadly, many changes are harmful.

All the time, more and more people are being born. These people need places to live and work, and they need food. For all these things people need land—land for factories and farms, for houses and roads. But when people take land for themselves, they destroy the homes of wild animals and plants. And even when people have enough land, they don't always look after it. They accidentally start forest fires. They dump litter without thinking. And they pollute the land and water with waste.

In a wild area, the number of plants and animals will stay about the same from year to year. The numbers may fall when people change the land. Many kinds of animals are now threatened and, without special care, some kinds will become extinct.

Before factories and cars, the air was much cleaner. When smoke rises from factory chimneys, some of the chemicals it contains are dissolved by moisture in the air. This turns the moisture into acid. Eventually, the moisture falls as rain. The acid raindrops harm plants. Trees, plants, and animals in lakes die.

A few thousand years ago, rain forests covered more than one-sixth of the world's land. Over half of these forests have been cut down.

People often spoil the land with their waste.

An explosion took place in 1986 at a nuclear power station at Chernobyl in Ukraine. A nuclear reactor— a device in which nuclear reactions take place—was destroyed, and harmful substances poured into the air. The winds carried the poisonous material, causing contaminated food and water supplies, as well as many health problems. Many people died as a result of the explosion. To prevent further contamination, the destroyed reactor was covered by a huge concrete and steel structure. The last working reactor at Chernobyl was shut down in 2000.

When accidents happen to oil tankers, oil spreads over the sea. Oil is also pumped into the sea when tankers and refineries are cleaned. The floating oil ruins beaches and kills wildlife, including many birds.

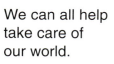

We can all help take care of our world.

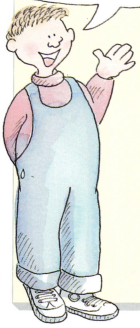

You can help

Some organizations are working to help save animals in danger. The World Wildlife Fund for Nature is one of these. In 1961, the Fund adopted a symbol—the giant panda of China. Fewer than one thousand giant pandas survive in the wild. With help from The World Wildlife Fund for Nature, the Chinese government is trying to save them.

Many countries have national parks, animal reserves, and other places where the land and the wildlife are protected. People everywhere can all help take care of the world. Groups of children often clean up litter left by careless visitors to beauty spots. Perhaps you can help keep the world beautiful near your home.

I'll see you soon

Ferdinand Magellan, a Portuguese sea captain, commanded the first expedition to sail around the world. The voyage took almost three years. It began in September 1519 and ended in September 1522. The first nonstop jet flight around the world was made in 1957. It took forty-five hours and nineteen minutes! By the mid-1970's, the supersonic Concorde could fly that distance in about seventeen hours!

When the explorer Christopher Columbus crossed the Atlantic Ocean in 1492, it took him a little over one month. In 1952, a ship, the *United States*, crossed the same ocean in less than three and a half days.

Long ago, wagons traveled at 3 miles (5 km) per hour. Today, a French train travels at 186 miles (301 km) per hour. The world seems a much smaller place than it did to our great-grandparents.

For a long time, people traveled mainly on foot. They learned to use animals to carry heavy loads.

Sailing ships helped people carry loads farther than before.

Today, jet airplanes can carry travelers faster than 550 miles (890 km) per hour.

By the end of the 1800's, steam trains could travel faster than 99 miles (160 km) per hour.

Getting the message

Sending messages is also easier today. How do you send a message? The simplest way is by talking, or if the person you want to speak to is a long way off, by shouting. But the sound of even the loudest shout doesn't travel far.

The Pony Express was used in North America between 1860 and 1861. Teams of riders carrying letters galloped between Missouri and California, a distance of 1,966 miles (3,164 km). Now e-mail can deliver a "letter" instantly!

Telephones allow us to speak to a friend on the next street or to a person on the other side of the world. The first telephone was invented in 1876 by a Scot who settled in the United States. His name was Alexander Graham Bell.

Many modern systems for sending messages around the world use communications satellites. These artificial satellites are in orbit around the earth. They pick up radio, telephone, television, and other signals beamed from transmitting stations on the ground. They send these signals back to any part of the world. People can watch an event on television at the same time it is taking place on the opposite side of the world.

Enjoy this book

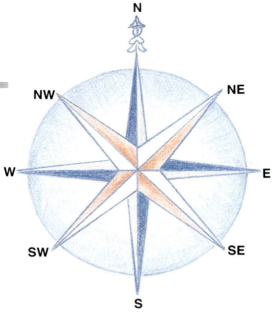

Have you ever dreamed of taking a trip around the world? How would you like to fly over the world's highest peak, Mount Everest? What about exploring unknown parts of the Amazon rain forest in South America? Would you like to drive over the high plains of Africa and see animals in the wild? How would you like to meet people in faraway countries and find out how they live?

The pages of this book are like a magic ticket. They will take you around the world without ever leaving home. Through maps and pictures, you will find out about the countries in fifteen regions of the world. You will be able to look at the land, the plants, the animals, the people and their work, and the major cities. Are you ready to start? Then let's go.

Maps tell people in which direction they are traveling. The main directions are north, south, east, and west. This drawing is a compass rose. The direction between north and east is called northeast. There are three other directions between the main directions.

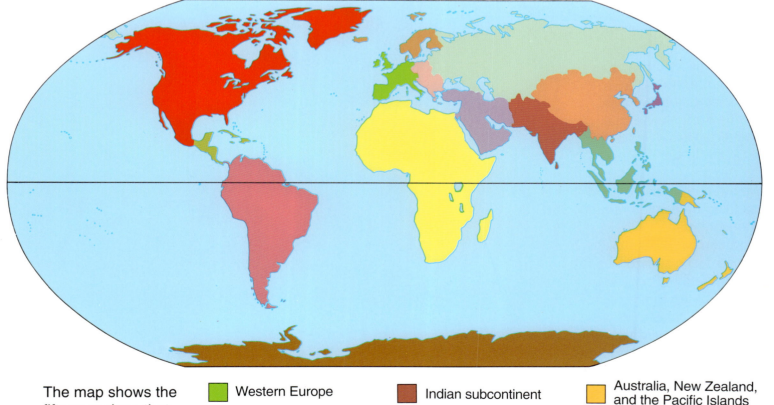

The map shows the fifteen regions that are described in this book. Each region has its own section filled with facts.

Western Europe

Northern Europe

Eastern Europe

Russia and its neighbors

Southwest Asia

Indian subcontinent

China and Eastern Asia

Japan

Southeast Asia

Africa

Australia, New Zealand, and the Pacific Islands

North America

Central America and the Caribbean Islands

South America

The cold lands

42

Each of the fifteen sections starts with a **Welcome** page. It gives you a quick idea of what to look for in the pages that follow.

The cities describes some of the cities in the region. You can find out about places in the cities that are of special interest to visitors.

The plants explains the kinds of plants found in the region.

The people tells about the people of the region, what they look like and how they live.

The land tells about mountains and plains, rivers and lakes, deserts and coral reefs, volcanoes and hot springs, and other land features.

The countries tells about the nations found in the region. The flags of countries discussed in the text are illustrated in this section.

The animals tells about the wildlife found in the region. The world's animals vary from place to place, just as the plants do.

Growing and making tells about some of the natural resources and industries of the region.

43

Welcome to Western Europe

Western Europe stretches from the large islands of Ireland and Britain to the southern parts of France and Italy on the Mediterranean Sea. Spain and Portugal reach out into the Atlantic Ocean to the west, and Western Europe almost touches Africa at the Rock of Gibraltar.

The region has thousands of miles of coastline and high mountain ranges, such as the Alps and the Pyrenees, which divide countries from each other. But the countries of Western Europe share many of the same plains, lakes, and rivers. Their people are used to moving freely across the region's borders and meeting for trade and pleasure. The countries of Western Europe are modern and industrialized and have come to depend upon each other in many ways.

There are many beautiful statues in Rome, the capital of Italy.

Vacationers learn to ski in the mountains of the Alps.

Equator

Many large castles stand along the Rhine River in Germany.

Tulips are gathered in the bulb fields of the Netherlands.

The Tower of London in the United Kingdom attracts many visitors.

Much of western Europe has rich farmland.

Steel is made in the industrial cities of many countries.

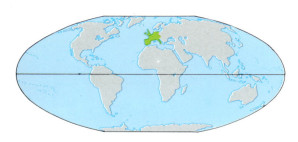

The countries

There are 18 nations in Western Europe. The United Kingdom, also called Britain, is really four countries—England, Northern Ireland, Scotland, and Wales—united under one government. Before World War II, there was a single country called Germany. After the war ended in 1945, Germany was divided and eventually became two separate countries, East Germany and West Germany. But in 1990, the two were once again united as a single nation.

Western Europe is one of the wealthiest and most powerful regions in the world. Many of its products travel by sea. Many countries have sea coasts. Others are linked by long, deep rivers. Barges carry goods back and forth along the rivers.

Most European countries belong to an organization called the European Union (EU). The EU promotes cooperation, in areas such as politics and economics, among member countries.

The history

Over 2,000 years ago the Roman Empire flourished in Western Europe. The Romans were skilled builders and engineers. They were also well-trained soldiers who conquered large areas of Africa and Asia.

Later, explorers and navigators from Western Europe traveled to most of the other regions of the world. Settlers from all over Western Europe went to live and work in these lands. Many became wealthy traders and sent exciting new foods and products to their home countries.

The two world wars caused great change in Western Europe. Many buildings were badly damaged by bombing, and millions of people died. When World War II was over, many towns were rebuilt.

The wealth

Since the 1800's, Western Europe has been a leading region in industry and manufacturing. It was the first area in the world to develop machines for use in factories. Today there are thousands of factories all over this region.

Western Europe needs large amounts of energy to help run its factories. This power is produced by the region's oil, coal, hydroelectric, and nuclear power stations.

Almost every piece of farmland in Western Europe is used. Many countries are able to supply much of their own produce, but some countries also import foods, such as grain and butter.

Western Europe is a wealthy and heavily populated region. Most people live in towns and cities. Although there is some unemployment, most people earn fairly good wages and live in comfortable homes.

The Colosseum in Rome, Italy, was built nearly 2,000 years ago by the Romans. It was a large outdoor theater.

46

Andorra   Austria   Belgium   France   Germany   Ireland   Italy   Liechtenstein

Luxembourg   Malta   Monaco

Netherlands   Portugal   San Marino

Spain   Switzerland   United Kingdom   Vatican City

Facts about Western Europe

There are eighteen countries in the region.

Area: 891,059 square miles (2,308,444 sq. km).

Population: About 354,212,000.

Highest mountain: Mont Blanc, on the border between France, Italy, and Switzerland, is 15,771 feet (4,807 m) high.

Longest river: The longest river completely inside Western Europe is the Rhine, which is about 820 miles (1,320 km) long.

Largest country: France.

Shannon

IRELAND   ■ Dublin

UNITED KINGDOM

North Sea

Thames

London ■

Elbe

Amsterdam ■
NETHERLANDS

Berlin ■

Brussels ■
BELGIUM

Rhine

GERMANY

LUXEMBOURG

Paris ■ *Seine*

Loire

Danube

Atlantic Ocean

FRANCE

Bern ■

LIECHTENSTEIN

Vienna ■

SWITZERLAND

AUSTRIA

Rhône

Po

PORTUGAL

MONACO ●

SAN MARINO ●

ANDORRA

Madrid ■

ITALY

■ Lisbon

Mediterranean Sea

SPAIN

Rome ■
VATICAN CITY

■ GIBRALTAR

The government

There are many types of governments in Western Europe. In most countries, there are several political parties. Adults vote for the party they want to form the government.

Some countries have a president who is head of state. Others, such as Spain and the United Kingdom, have a king or queen who is head of state.

● MALTA

Looking at the land

Western Europe has several high mountain ranges. They include the Pyrenees on France's border with Spain and the snow-capped Alps. It is difficult for people to cross the Pyrenees with goods to trade. As a result, France and Spain have had to trade with each other mainly by sea for many years. The Alps are the largest mountain range in Western Europe. Glaciers lie near the mountaintops.

Some of the region's longest rivers have their sources in the Alps. The Rhine River begins as two rushing streams that spill down a mountainside, then flow into Lake Constance in Switzerland. From there the Rhine runs through France, Germany, and the Netherlands before entering the North Sea.

Western Europe has a rugged coastline. The land curves in and out, forming many natural harbors that are important to the fishing industry. Off the coast lie many islands.

The **Alps** form a huge mountain system that runs through many of the countries of Western Europe. The highest peaks are often snow-capped. They tower over narrow, fertile valleys. The valleys are passes through the mountains. Roads and railways go through them. Mountain climbing is popular in the Alps.

Much of the coast of Western Europe faces the Atlantic Ocean. Powerful waves have worn away the rocks and carved bays in the coastline. The coast of **Brittany** in France is especially rugged, with jagged cliffs and sandy inlets.

The **Rhine** is Europe's most important inland waterway. It flows from the high Alps to the North Sea. As the Rhine crosses Germany, it flows over wide plains and through narrow gorges. Here, grand old castles overlook the river. They were built many centuries ago as fortresses.

Much of the **Netherlands** is below sea level. Long canals crisscross the Netherlands. They have been dug to drain water from the flat, low-lying land. Without the canals, large areas of land would be flooded by rain.

Netherlands

Rhine

Atlantic Ocean

Brittany

Lake Constance

Alps

Pyrenees

Rock of Gibraltar

Gibraltar lies on a narrow strip of land that juts out from southern Spain. It is crowned by a huge limestone cliff, called the **Rock of Gibraltar.** It overlooks the Strait of Gibraltar, a narrow strip of sea.

Plants and animals

edelweiss

golden eagle

chamois

alpine ibex

gentian

mountain avens

marmot

purple saxifrage

A rich tangle of flowers grows in old meadows and along paths in Western Europe. Yellow buttercups and red poppies stand out among the grasses, where harvest mice weave nests and the tiny wren searches for insects.

Western Europe was once covered with woods and marshes. But over many hundreds of years, most of the woods were chopped down and the marshes drained. The land was used for farming and for houses and factories. People brought sheep, horses, and cows to graze on the cleared land. Larger wild animals had nowhere to live and soon died out. But smaller animals, such as foxes and badgers, still survive—sometimes close to towns.

wren

white dead nettle

field mouse

dog rose

honeysuckle

common fescue grass

foxglove

common rough grass

buttercup

red poppy

common meadow grass

burdock

dandelion

cow parsley

mole

rabbit

clover

Mountain

Below the snowy peaks of the Alps, the thin soil is covered with grasses and some flowers. Alpine ibex and chamois climb easily over the rocky slopes. Golden eagles search the mountainsides for small animals.

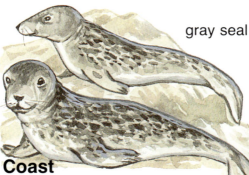

gray seal

Coast

On rocky shores, the oyster catcher feeds on shellfish, and shore crabs hide in bladderwrack on the beach. Off the Atlantic coast, gray seals rest on rocks.

bladderwrack

Meadow

Many kinds of grasses grow in the meadow. Among the grasses there are wild flowers. Butterflies visit the flowers to feed on nectar. Rabbits and moles burrow in the soil.

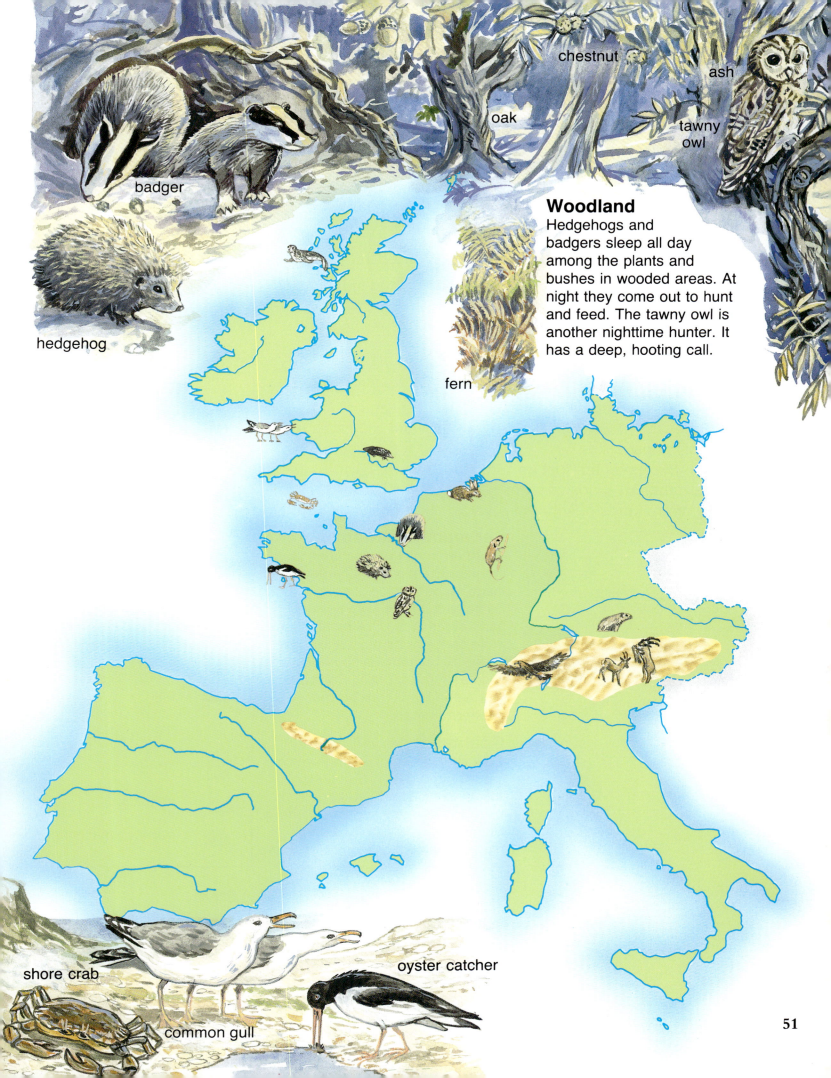

badger

chestnut

ash

oak

tawny
owl

hedgehog

Woodland

Hedgehogs and
badgers sleep all day
among the plants and
bushes in wooded areas. At
night they come out to hunt
and feed. The tawny owl is
another nighttime hunter. It
has a deep, hooting call.

fern

shore crab

oyster catcher

common gull

Growing and making

Through the hot glare from the blast furnace, the steelworker watches the huge ladle fill with white-hot liquid iron. When the ladle is full, the worker signals for it to move slowly forward until it tilts. The liquid iron is then poured into the round opening of another furnace. The melted iron spits and hisses as it splashes into the furnace. Gases are thrown up in a huge yellow flame. When the furnace is full, the iron will be made into steel.

Steel is one of the most important industries in Western Europe. Steel is used to make machinery and cars. Large supplies of raw materials such as coal, iron ore, and gas are found under the ground. These provide fuel and materials for all sorts of industries.

Western Europe is not just an industrial region. Farming is also important. All kinds of crops can be grown because there are many kinds of soil and a variety of climates.

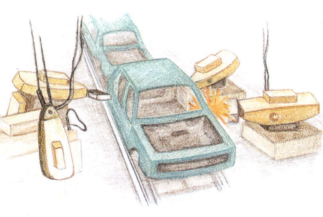

Car manufacturing
There are many car factories in Western Europe. Most cars are made on production lines. Sometimes robots help assemble parts of the cars. This means that more cars can be built at lower prices. Many famous sports cars, such as Ferrari, BMW, Porsche, and Aston Martin are built in Western Europe.

Coal mining
Coal mining has been an important industry in Western Europe for many years. There are large coal fields in Germany and Great Britain. Some coal is dug from open-pit mines, but most of the coal is found deep under the ground.

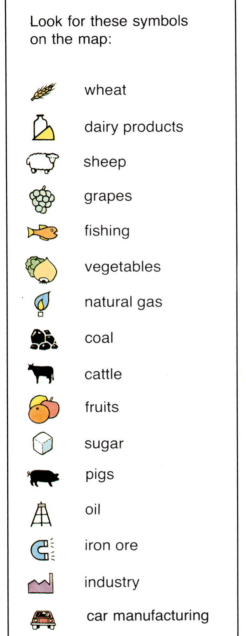

Look for these symbols on the map:

- wheat
- dairy products
- sheep
- grapes
- fishing
- vegetables
- natural gas
- coal
- cattle
- fruits
- sugar
- pigs
- oil
- iron ore
- industry
- car manufacturing

Steel
Steel is one of the most important industries in Western Europe. Steel is used to make machinery and cars.

Grapes

Grapes are grown in vineyards. There are many parts of Western Europe where the soil and the climate are just right for growing grapes. Some are sold for eating, but most German, French, and Italian grapes are pressed, or squashed, and made into wine. The wine is sold all over the world.

Fishing

Around the Mediterranean Sea and the Atlantic Ocean there are many fishing towns and villages. Fleets of fishing boats catch many kinds of fish, such as cod and herring. Some are sold fresh as soon as the catch is landed. Some are frozen. Others, such as sardines, are taken to canning factories where they are cooked and packed in cans with sauce or vegetable oil.

Farming

Many Western European farmers grow crops such as fruit, grain, and vegetables. There are also many livestock farmers who keep pigs, cattle, and sheep for their meat and wool. Dairy farmers keep cows for milk and dairy products.

People and how they live

Western Europe is one of the world's liveliest centers of art and culture. Throughout the year, festivals and carnivals take place, both in the towns and countryside, to mark special days and events. There are also art, music, and film exhibits.

Several countries in Western Europe still have a king or queen. Many royal ceremonies that have been carried on for hundreds of years take place each year. Children here learn about their country's history and traditions in school. This knowledge often continues to play its part in their daily lives as they grow up. Western European architects, fashion designers, and engineers are famous throughout the world for their modern designs, yet they respect the ideas of the past.

In summer, some Swiss farmers leave their homes in the valleys to drive their cattle up the mountainside. There, the farmers live in log cabins while the cattle graze in the pastures.

Soccer is a popular sport throughout Western Europe. Each team has its own colors, and the team supporters dress up in scarves and hats to show which team they support.

All these people live in Western Europe.

Each year a procession of ox-drawn wagons, riders on horseback, and trudging pilgrims enters the village of El Rocio in southern Spain. This religious festival celebrates the discovery of a holy statue over 300 years ago.

In some parts of Ireland, people still live in traditional cottages. Many of the cottages are painted white and have thatched roofs made of straw or reeds.

French people are famous for their cooking and for creating dishes that are copied in many parts of the world. There are many delicious foods on sale at the restaurants. Diners also eat outside at sidewalk cafes. They may get some live entertainment, too!

Thousands of people from India, Pakistan, and the West Indies now live in Britain. They have brought with them many of their own customs. Indian restaurants are now common in most British towns. West Indians in London organize a colorful carnival every year.

The cities

Western Europe has some of the world's most famous cities. If you want to go shopping in Venice, Italy, you may go by boat. This city has streets full of water. Venice is built on many small islands in a shallow lagoon. Paris, the capital city of France, has been a center of art and learning for centuries. And London, in England, is one of the world's oldest and most historic cities.

The cities of Western Europe are visited by people from all over the world who come to admire the architecture of old palaces and cathedrals. Museums and galleries contain huge collections of art from the past. But most cities have many new buildings, too. Modern department stores and offices stand next to houses and churches that are hundreds of years old.

⇧
Until 1989, the German city of **Berlin** was divided by the Berlin Wall. East Berlin was controlled by Communist East Germany, and West Berlin by democratic West Germany. But the wall was taken down in 1989. In this photo, happy Berliners, smiling and waving sparklers from the top of the Berlin Wall, are celebrating the opening up of their city.

⇐ The canals of **Venice,** in northern Italy, make the city very attractive, but they also cause problems. During winter storms, high tides cause serious flooding.

Europoort is the largest artificial harbor in the world. It is built on the coast of the Netherlands and is the port of the city of Rotterdam. Europoort handles huge ships carrying grain and oil. It has oil refineries, factories, and metal foundries. Europoort is sometimes called "The Gateway to Europe." ➭

London is the capital city of the United Kingdom. The City of London is London's oldest area. The huge round roof of Saint Paul's Cathedral towers over the other buildings. The River Thames is the most famous and most important river in England. ⬇⬇

There are many famous landmarks in **Paris,** but the easiest to spot is the Eiffel Tower, which stands high above the city. It was built to celebrate the World's Fair in 1889. ➭

Through Europe by truck

The truck pulls slowly out of the yard. It is loaded with crates of carefully packed oranges. They are juicy and sweet. They have been grown on the Costa Blanca coast and have ripened in the hot Spanish sun. Valencia oranges are among the most popular in the world. Now they are on their way from the packing yard in Valencia to the city of Amsterdam in the Netherlands. The journey will take two days as the truck crosses northern Spain, then France, Belgium, and the Netherlands.

Once out of the busy city of Valencia, the truck makes its way to the autopista, or expressway. It is a long, fast, two- or three-lane road. Payments, called tolls, must be paid along the way. The autopista passes by Barcelona, Spain's number-one industrial city.

European expressways are crowded in the summer as people leave the cities for vacations in the countryside or along the sea coast.

58

At Avignon there is a famous bridge that was built by the Romans almost two thousand years ago.

North of Barcelona is the border between Spain and France. The driver takes the famous Autoroute du Soleil through France to Paris. On the way, the truck passes the cities of Nîmes and Avignon.

It is late when the truck nears Paris. The driver pulls off the autoroute and into a huge rest area where there is a gas station, restaurant, and a hotel. The rest area is near the town of Fontainebleau, where there is a beautiful royal palace.

The next morning, the driver sets off for Paris. The Eiffel Tower rises in the distance. The ring road around the city is jammed with morning traffic, and it is an hour before the truck is through the city and heading northward.

The truck heads north across a vast stretch of flat land known as the Great European Plain, where it enters Belgium. Brussels, Belgium's capital, is the home of the European Union. Here, representatives of all the member countries meet to discuss their cooperation in matters such as economics, law enforcement, and foreign policy. Once past Brussels, the end of the journey is near. The driver points the truck toward Amsterdam and looks forward to a well-earned rest.

Amsterdam at last! The truck will be unloaded quickly and the oranges sold in supermarkets. In exchange, the truck will be loaded with a container of wheat to take to the flour mills of Spain. Spain has plenty of oranges, but it buys wheat from its European neighbors. Many of the countries of Europe are working together to form one large community in which they can buy and sell goods freely to one another.

Journeys like this are happening all the time on Europe's busy expressways. Thousands of trucks crisscross Europe every day, carrying goods to where they are needed.

Now there is time to relax. The driver may stroll beside some of Amsterdam's many canals or have coffee at a roadside café.

59

Welcome to Northern Europe

Northern Europe is a cold, icy region that lies partly within the Arctic Circle. It is almost completely surrounded by sea, except where it joins Germany and Russia. Parts of Northern Europe are covered with large forests of evergreen trees. Other parts, like Denmark, have low-lying areas where people farm. Most of the countries' industries are in the big cities near the coasts.

The northern part of Norway is often called "the land of the midnight sun." For ten weeks in the summer months, the sun shines day and night. This twenty-four hour daylight is caused by the tilt of the earth, which brings the North Pole closer to the sun. The people enjoy this short but warm summer and spend the long evenings out of doors. In winter, the days are short and dark.

Equator

Fiords are narrow inlets of the sea.

Reindeer eat grass in summer and moss in winter.

Sweden is one of the world's largest producers of paper.

Forests of evergreen trees provide timber for homes.

The seas of Northern Europe have many kinds of fish.

Hot springs are found in volcanic areas of Iceland.

Tivoli Gardens is a famous amusement park in Copenhagen.

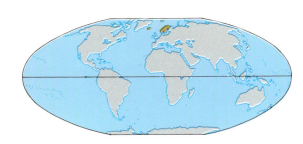

The countries

Northern Europe is made up of five independent countries. These are Denmark, Finland, Iceland, Norway, and Sweden. Iceland is an island in the North Atlantic Ocean to the west of Norway. To the east of Finland lies Russia. To the south of Denmark is Germany.

The northernmost parts of this region lie within the Arctic Circle. The winters are very long. There is much ice and snow, and the days are short.

The history

The people of these countries have always depended on the sea for their living. Around the year A.D. 800, people called Vikings lived in Northern Europe. They were adventurous sailors who traveled along the coasts of Europe in their long ships. They often raided settlements and towns, carrying off slaves and treasure. They also traded with other nations. It is thought that Viking ships sailed as far as North America.

Today these five countries have close and friendly links with each other. But this has not always been so. For many years Sweden and Denmark fought one another. Sweden also fought against Russia to determine which nation should rule Finland.

The Vikings were fierce warriors and pirates who lived in Northern Europe from the A.D. 800's onward. They were skilled sailors. Their ships were called long ships.

The wealth

The countries of Northern Europe have always relied on the sea to provide fish to eat and for export. Fishing is so important to Iceland that a serious quarrel arose in the past between the fishermen of Iceland and Great Britain. The Icelanders believed that the British fishing fleets were fishing in Icelandic waters. Both sides had to make an agreement to fish only in their own areas.

Norway is one of the largest oil producers in Europe. Sweden exports large amounts of iron ore. But the other countries of Northern Europe have few natural resources, such as fuel or minerals. Electrical power, which is produced by running water, is important. Most Northern European countries import fuels and minerals from the rest of the world. They pay for these imports by trading in timber, dairy products, fish, and manufactured goods.

ICELAND
Lake Mývatn
Reykjavík

Denmark　Finland　Iceland　Norway　Sweden

The government

Denmark, Sweden, and Norway are monarchies. The head of state in these countries is a king or queen. But the countries are governed by a prime minister and an elected parliament.

Iceland and Finland are republics. Their heads of state are called presidents. Each republic also has a prime minister and a parliament.

Most of the people of this region earn high wages and have a comfortable way of life.

FINLAND

SWEDEN

Gulf of Bothnia

NORWAY

Oslo

Klarälven

Helsinki

Stockholm

Lake Vänern

Göta älv

North Sea

DENMARK

Copenhagen

Baltic Sea

Facts about Northern Europe

There are five countries in the region.
Area: 507,186 square miles (1,313,524 sq. km).
Population: About 24,208,000.
Largest country: Sweden.
Highest mountain: Galdhøpiggen, in Norway, is 8,100 feet (2,469 m) high.
Longest river: Klarälven-Göta älv, in southern Sweden, is about 447 miles (720 km) long.

63

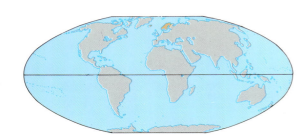

Looking at the land

Much of the land of Northern Europe is made up of rugged mountains overlooking a jagged coastline. Many thousands of years ago, huge ice sheets and rivers of ice called glaciers covered this area. As the glaciers slowly moved down to the sea, they wore out deep narrow valleys and hollows called fiords.

The landscape of the northernmost region is very dramatic. Iceland is sometimes called "the land of frost and fire." In many parts, volcanoes erupt, and hot springs and geysers spout steam into the cold air. Huge waterfalls tumble down the southern mountains of Norway, and farther north, glaciers carve their way to the Arctic seas. Thousands of rocky islands lie off the Norwegian coast, where they are battered by rough waves.

Deep sea inlets cut into the coastline of Norway. These steep-sided waterways are called fiords. They were carved out by glaciers more than 10,000 years ago when the climate was much colder than it is today. **Geiranger Fiord,** in the western part of the country, is one of the most beautiful places on Norway's coast.

Much of **Denmark** is fertile farming land where dairy cattle graze and pigs are raised. The gently rolling hills, green pasture, and flower-filled meadows are very beautiful and quite unlike the rugged land farther north.

Lake Mývatn

Iceland

Lake Mývatn is in northern Iceland. Around the lake are volcanoes and hot, steamy springs. The water in these springs is heated by hot rock that lies under the surface of the earth. Scientists think that Iceland was formed by several small volcanic islands. Lava gradually filled in the seas between these islands.

The **Gulf of Bothnia** is in the northernmost part of the Baltic Sea. In winter, it freezes over. Only icebreakers can make their way along the icy coast of Sweden.

Gulf of Bothnia

Finland

Geiranger Fiord

Denmark

Baltic Sea

Finland has about 60,000 lakes. Most are in the south. There are small, rocky islands in many of the lakes. About 20,000 years ago, Finland was covered by ice. The moving ice wore out many hollows in the land. When the ice melted, water filled the hollows to form the lakes.

Plants and animals

dwarf birch

sedge

whooper swan

long-tailed duck

rush

goldeneye

The conifer forests of Northern Europe have to survive long, cold winters with heavy snow. The needlelike leaves of the pine trees that grow here stand up well to freezing gales. The snow easily slides off these tall trees. Most of the forest animals have thick fur for protection against the cold. The bearlike wolverine has long, shiny fur and large, hairy feet to help it run on firm snow. The capercaillie is a large forest bird. Its feet have a fringe of feathers that act like snowshoes in the winter.

Northern Europe still has many great forests. But in the far north, only mosses, lichens, and dwarf plants can survive. Here, vast numbers of insects provide food for birds during the short summer. Deep inlets and steep cliffs make fine nesting places for migrating birds along the beautiful coastline.

Norway spruce

crested tit

Scots pine

Tengmalm's owl

Mountain birchwood

Roe deer feed on leaves and herbs and chew the bark of the birch trees. Shrews hunt ground insects, and bluethroats nest here. The rare European beaver lives near water.

birch

wood sorrel

wolverine

capercaillie

roe deer

Conifer forest

The wolverine hunts in Norway's spruce and pine forests. It can swim and it climbs trees easily. The pine marten is an even better climber when it wants to catch birds. It also hunts the wood lemmings that live on the forest floor. Owls make their nests in the trees.

pine marten

wood lemming

beaver

shrew

66

Iceland

Lake Mývatn

Lake Mývatn is in northern Iceland. Around the lake are volcanoes and hot, steamy springs. The water in these springs is heated by hot rock that lies under the surface of the earth. Scientists think that Iceland was formed by several small volcanic islands. Lava gradually filled in the seas between these islands.

The **Gulf of Bothnia** is in the northernmost part of the Baltic Sea. In winter, it freezes over. Only icebreakers can make their way along the icy coast of Sweden.

Gulf of Bothnia

Finland

Geiranger Fiord

Denmark

Baltic Sea

Finland has about 60,000 lakes. Most are in the south. There are small, rocky islands in many of the lakes. About 20,000 years ago, Finland was covered by ice. The moving ice wore out many hollows in the land. When the ice melted, water filled the hollows to form the lakes.

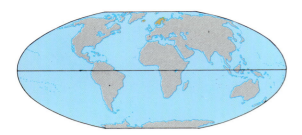

Plants and animals

dwarf birch

whooper swan

sedge

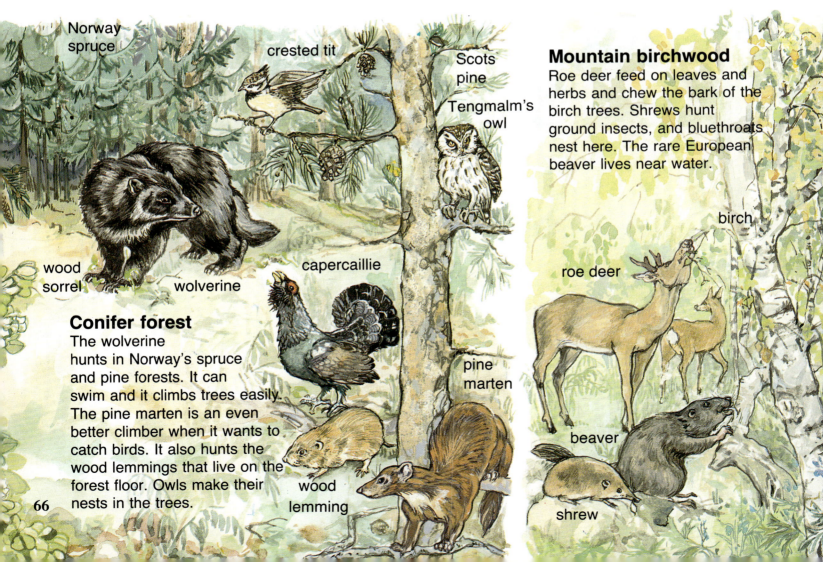

long-tailed duck

rush

goldeneye

The conifer forests of Northern Europe have to survive long, cold winters with heavy snow. The needlelike leaves of the pine trees that grow here stand up well to freezing gales. The snow easily slides off these tall trees. Most of the forest animals have thick fur for protection against the cold. The bearlike wolverine has long, shiny fur and large, hairy feet to help it run on firm snow. The capercaillie is a large forest bird. Its feet have a fringe of feathers that act like snowshoes in the winter.

Northern Europe still has many great forests. But in the far north, only mosses, lichens, and dwarf plants can survive. Here, vast numbers of insects provide food for birds during the short summer. Deep inlets and steep cliffs make fine nesting places for migrating birds along the beautiful coastline.

Norway spruce

crested tit

Scots pine

Tengmalm's owl

Mountain birchwood
Roe deer feed on leaves and herbs and chew the bark of the birch trees. Shrews hunt ground insects, and bluethroats nest here. The rare European beaver lives near water.

birch

wood sorrel

wolverine

capercaillie

roe deer

pine marten

Conifer forest
The wolverine hunts in Norway's spruce and pine forests. It can swim and it climbs trees easily. The pine marten is an even better climber when it wants to catch birds. It also hunts the wood lemmings that live on the forest floor. Owls make their nests in the trees.

beaver

wood lemming

shrew

66

arctic tern

Coast and fiord
Eider ducks dive for mussels
and other shellfish. Arctic terns
nest on the shore. They fly
all the way from the Antarctic to
nest here each spring. White-
tailed eagles build large nests
on cliffs or in pines.

otter

white-
tailed
eagle

eider duck

Iceland
Thick layers of flies hover over
the surface of Iceland's lakes in
summer. Long-tailed ducks
scoop them up. Whooper swans
nest in the reed beds and on
small islands. Their long necks
allow them to feed on
underwater plants. Goldeneye
ducks, from North America, also
nest here.

arctic
salmon

woolly
willow

rough-legged
buzzard

bluethroat

short-eared owl

rush

ptarmigan

Lapland moors
Woolly willows and rushes grow
in damp areas. The ptarmigan,
whose feathers turn white in
winter, feeds on berries. Blue
hares also turn white in winter.
These animals hide easily from
their enemies in the snow.
Rough-legged buzzards and
short-eared owls fly low, hunting
for voles.

blue hare

monkshood

vole

crowberry

Growing and making

The workers look anxiously at the sky. They hope the weather will be good and the sea calm. At a given signal, several small tugs start their engines and begin to tow the huge oil platforms out to sea from Stavanger harbor. Far out in the North Sea, the platform will be anchored to the seabed. The oil workers will drill down to bring up the oil that lies in rocks under the sea.

Norway has many oil rigs and drills that locate natural gas in the North Sea. There is enough oil and gas for all of Norway's needs and still a lot left to export to other countries.

Northern Europe depends on the sea for its oil and its fish. Mining, growing timber, and farming are also important to some countries. The fast-flowing rivers provide hydroelectric power for use in industry.

Oil in Norway
One of Norway's most valuable resources lies under the sea. Most of the oil that Norway gets from the North Sea is exported to other countries.

Forestry in Finland
Finland has many forests of trees such as spruce, pine, birch, and fir. Forest workers are busy all year, planting young saplings, caring for the growing trees, and felling large trees in winter.

Look for these symbols on the map:

🐄	cattle
	dairy products
🌲	timber
🐟	fishing
🐖	pigs
	oil
	natural gas
	iron ore
	copper
	industry
🚗	car manufacturing
⚡	hydroelectricity

Mining in Sweden
Sweden is a leading producer of iron ore. The mountains of Kiruna, in the north of Sweden, are rich in this mineral. The iron ore is heated in blast furnaces until it becomes a liquid. Then it is made into steel.

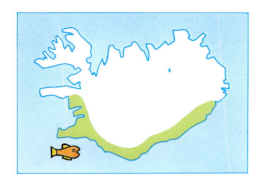

Hydroelectric power in Norway

Norway's fast-flowing rivers are used to make hydroelectric power. This helps to run the factories where such things as aluminum and fertilizer are made. Electric power is also used to heat people's houses. Norway has almost no coal to use as fuel.

Fishing in Iceland

The fishing fleets of Iceland catch large amounts of cod and herring. These are frozen for people to eat or turned into fish meal or fish oil to be fed to animals or used in fertilizer.

Dairy farming in Denmark

Denmark is the only country in Northern Europe with much farmland. Most of the farms are small. There are large herds of dairy cattle that provide milk. Some of the milk is made into cheese and butter.

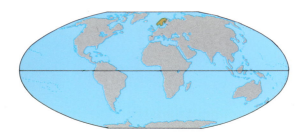

People and how they live

In the far north of Europe, the winter days are very short. Deep snow may cover the ground for months at a time, and it is often very cold. It's so difficult to travel that the children find it easier to ski to school. Once indoors they have no trouble keeping warm. Most Northern European countries are very mountainous, and rushing mountain rivers and waterfalls provide electric power to heat homes and factories.

During the warmer months, many people who live on the coast or in the fiords use their own small motorboats to travel from place to place. The lakes are wonderful places for rowing and yachting. Many tourists arrive, often by sea. They join local vacationers visiting historic cities, such as Oslo and Copenhagen, touring the fiords by steamer or camping by the lakes.

In some parts of Iceland, water that has been heated far below the earth's crust bubbles to the surface and collects in pools. The water contains minerals that are known to help ease painful diseases. People relax and swim in the warm waters.

Many children in Northern Europe learn to ski when they are very young. Cross-country skiing is one of the most popular sports. Schools have a short vacation in the middle of winter, and many families go to the mountains to ski.

Steamers carry passengers up and down the fiords to enjoy the breathtaking views.

On June 21, which is Midsummer's Day, there are celebrations all over Sweden. Tall maypoles are put up in each village. The poles are decorated with leaves and flowers, and people dance around them.

The Sami live in the far north of Norway, Sweden, Finland, and part of Russia. Many live in towns and villages. But some still live as nomads, herding reindeer across the snows in search of pasture-land. They raise reindeer for meat, milk, and skins.

All these people live in Northern Europe.

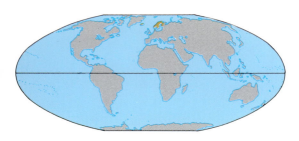

The cities

The ports of Northern Europe are busy twenty-four hours a day. At dawn, the first fishing boats come in to unload the morning catch. Large container ships carrying goods to and from all parts of the world may be entering the dock, too. Some carry supplies that must be lifted from the hold by crane. Others carry food and goods for the drilling platforms that are working hundreds of miles (kilometers) out to sea in the North Sea and Norwegian Sea oilfields. The ports are very important to the life of the region. Because inland areas are mountainous, most goods and people travel by sea.

The largest cities of Northern Europe are all busy ports. Most people today live in the cities and towns of the region and not in the countryside. Many of the city streets are lined with striking new buildings.

Finland's capital city, **Helsinki,** has wide streets and modern buildings. The main cathedral overlooks the city harbor. Helsinki has a large, busy port. In the coldest winters, the port is sometimes closed because of ice.

Reykjavík is the capital city and chief seaport of Iceland. Its name means "smoking bay." This is because of the steam rising from volcanic hot springs nearby. Spring water is used to heat buildings.

⇑

Stavanger is one of the busiest towns in Norway. It is an important base for the country's oil industry in the North Sea. In the shipyards of Stavanger, ocean-drilling platforms and oil tankers are built.

Stockholm was once a fortress on an island in a lake. The settlement grew and spread to other islands. Today, Stockholm is built on both sides of the lake, around the old town. It is a major center of industry. ⇓

⇑

Oslo is Norway's largest city. Along the main avenue in the city center are the royal palace, the parliament building, the cathedral, and old university buildings. Most people live in the suburbs among forests and lakes.

Welcome to Eastern Europe

Eastern Europe stretches from Poland on the northern Baltic Sea southward through Romania and Bulgaria along the Black Sea all the way to Greece in the sunny Mediterranean. Some countries in this area, including the Czech Republic, Slovakia, Hungary, and Macedonia, have no coast. They are completely surrounded by land. One of the largest rivers in Europe, the Danube, flows across many countries of the region. This busy waterway is used by cargo boats.

Mountains cover much of Eastern Europe. The Carpathian range extends between Slovakia and Poland into Romania. Other mountain groups stretch across parts of Slovenia, Croatia, Bosnia-Herzegovina, Serbia and Montenegro, Albania, Macedonia, and Greece. Hundreds of small islands that lie off the mainland of Greece have become popular vacation resorts. Farmers grow crops on fertile plains in Poland and other parts of Eastern Europe. Poland is also known for its industries.

Temple ruins show where the ancient Greeks worshiped over 2,000 years ago.

Equator

Family life is important to many Eastern Europeans.

People like to decorate fabrics with colorful embroidery.

Huge container ships and tankers are built in Poland.

Vacation resorts on the Greek islands are very popular.

Some ways of farming have remained the same for hundreds of years.

The Old Town of Prague has changed very little in 500 years.

75

The countries

This region is made up of thirteen countries. These include Albania, Bulgaria, the Czech Republic, Greece, Hungary, Poland, Romania, and Slovakia (which used to be joined with the Czech Republic as Czechoslovakia). Eastern Europe also includes five countries that once formed Yugoslavia. They are Bosnia-Herzegovina, Croatia, Macedonia, Serbia and Montenegro, and Slovenia.

Countries in Eastern Europe lie to the east of Germany and to the west of Russia. After World War II (1939–1945), Communist governments ran all these countries, except for Greece.

In 1989, the people of Bulgaria, Czechoslovakia, Hungary, Poland, and Romania forced their leaders from power. They formed new governments. In 1990, the Communist Party in Yugoslavia lost power. Strong independence movements in the Yugoslav states resulted in civil war. But the division of Czechoslovakia in 1993 was peaceful.

The history

For centuries, Eastern Europe has been an unstable part of the world. The region was invaded by many nations, and the rulers often quarreled among themselves. During World War I (1914–1918) and World War II (1939–1945), many of the countries suffered great damage. Whole towns and cities were destroyed. After World War II, much rebuilding work was needed.

For many years, there was very little contact between the Communist countries of Eastern Europe and the rest of the world. Today, all the European countries are becoming more dependent upon each other.

Many people now live in Eastern Europe's cities, which have grown quickly since the 1940's.

The wealth

The countries of Eastern Europe do not have as much industrial wealth or power as those of Western Europe. Many factories don't have the most modern machines. This means that goods are often produced at a slow rate.

Although there are large areas of fertile farmland in Eastern Europe, the harvests are not large. In some places the farmers' ways of working are traditional and slow.

In many of the countries, the Communist governments owned most of the farmland. Many of these farms were called collectives. The workers on the collectives shared in the profits if the harvest was very good. Today, private persons own most of the farmland.

Albania

Bosnia-Herzegovina

Bulgaria

Croatia

Czech Republic

Greece

Hungary

Macedonia

Poland

Romania

Serbia and Montenegro

Slovakia

Slovenia

Baltic Sea

Vistula

■ Warsaw

P O L A N D

■ Prague

CZECH REPUBLIC

SLOVAKIA

● Bratislava

Danube

■ Budapest

HUNGARY

Lake Balaton

Ljubljana

SLOVENIA

■ Zagreb

CROATIA

Sava

BOSNIA-HERZEGOVINA

Sarajevo ■

Adriatic Sea

SERBIA AND MONTENEGRO

● Belgrade

R O M A N I A

● Bucharest ■

Danube

■ Sofia

BULGARIA

Black Sea

■ Skopje

MACEDONIA

■ Tiranë

ALBANIA

GREECE

Aegean Sea

Ionian Sea

■ Athens

Mediterranean Sea

Facts about Eastern Europe

There are thirteen countries in the region.

Area: 501,350 square miles (1,298,490 sq. km).

Population: About 131,100,000.

Largest country: Poland.

Highest mountain: Musala Peak in Bulgaria is 9,596 feet (2,925 m) high.

Longest river: The Danube, which runs from Germany through Austria and Eastern Europe to the Black Sea, is 1,777 miles (2,860 km) long.

77

Looking at the land

Eastern Europe is a fertile region. It has a mild climate and enough rainfall to help crops grow well. Where the land is flat, the rain collects in rivers that crisscross the landscape. For centuries, these waterways have been used by large boats to carry cargo. The Danube is Eastern Europe's major river. It flows from Germany to its delta on the Black Sea. At its delta, the river widens into a huge maze of channels and lakes that wind through tall reeds and grasses.

North of the Danube are the Carpathian Mountains. These include several ranges along Slovakia's border with Poland. In the south of the region is the rugged Balkan Peninsula. *Balkan* is a Turkish word that means "mountain." The peninsula juts into the Mediterranean Sea, and much of its coastline is dotted with tiny islands.

The flat plains and gently rolling hills of **Poland** are crisscrossed with rivers. The longest river is the Vistula. This is Poland's major farming area.

Postojna cave is one of the many caves in the mountains of western Slovenia. The Pivka River flows through the caves, wearing away the limestone rock. Hanging from the roofs of the caves are long, stone "icicles," called stalactites. Rising from the floor are stony stumps called stalagmites. They are made by water containing lime, which has dripped from the roof for many hundreds of years.

The **Danube** begins as a small river in Germany. As it flows through Hungary, it becomes deep and wide and fast-flowing. Finally, as it nears the Black Sea, the river flows more slowly across a wide plain.

The **Carpathian Mountains** stretch between Slovakia and Poland into Romania. Here there are lakes and forests. The land in the mountain valleys is fertile.

Poland

Vistula

Carpathian Mountains

Postojna cave

Carpathian Mountains

Danube

Black Sea

Mount Olympus

Mount Olympus is 9,570 feet (2,917 m) high. It is the highest mountain in Greece. The ancient Greeks thought that the gods lived on this mountain. They believed that Zeus, father of all the gods, sat on his throne at the top.

Mediterranean Sea

79

Plants and animals

reed mace

In the northern part of this region there is a stretch of thick forest. Here, huge old trees reach toward the sky. Alongside them, tiny shoots spring from the ground. And trees at the very end of their lives lie rotting and covered with moss. Many animals live in the forest. Wild boars search for fungi, called truffles, which grow underground near the roots of trees. Squirrels and woodpeckers make their nests in the branches. And lynxes move quietly through the forest in search of food.

Farther south, areas of marsh are home to many water birds that nest in the tall reeds. Parts of the Carpathian Mountains are covered with grasses and flowering plants. These attract a variety of butterflies. In the warm south, the plants and animals must survive long, hot summers and strong, dry winds.

purple heron

reed warbler

Forest
The wild boar and the lynx are two of the largest animals living in the broad-leaved forests.

Marsh
Hidden by the reeds at the edge of the water, avocets and purple herons feed. They have long legs to wade through the water. Herons spear fish with their long bills. Reed warblers weave their nests into the tall reeds that grow on the marshy land.

red squirrel

birch

walnut

sycamore

beech

woodpecker

hazel

lynx

fern

wild boar

elm

truffle

beetle

wood ant

bat

olm

cave spider

Cave
Bats, cave spiders, and creatures called olms live in some of Eastern Europe's cool, dark caves. Olms have eellike bodies and live in underground lakes and streams.

clouded
yellow
butterfly

Hungarian
glider

reed

avocet

beech

spruce

pine

Mountain
The smooth, rounded Carpathian
Mountains are covered with alpine
flowers and mosses. The clouded
yellow butterfly and the Hungarian
glider get nectar from the flowers.
Forests of pine, spruce, and
beech grow on the lower slopes.

oak
tree

olive tree

Coast
Snakes and lizards live
near the warm Mediterranean
coast. They bask on rocks
during the day. At night they
crawl under stones and into
holes to keep warm. Inland,
there are olive and oak trees.
Their waxy leaves prevent the
plant's moisture from
evaporating in the hot sun.

lizard

viper

81

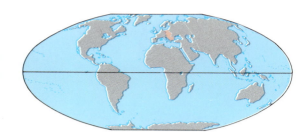

Growing and making

The glassmaker breathes in deeply then starts to blow very gently into the long, iron blowpipe. The pipe is about five feet (1.5 m) long, and on its far end hangs a small glistening drop of liquid glass. Slowly, the glass drop begins to bulge. It grows and grows into a hollow bulb or balloon shape.

The Czech Republic produces some of the world's most beautiful glassware. Much of the glass is made in a region called Bohemia, which has been famous for its glass for centuries.

Eastern Europe is rich in minerals. Poland is one of the leading coal-mining countries of the world. Bauxite is mined in Serbia and Montenegro, Croatia, and Hungary. Oil and gas are important in Romania. Many new industries have been set up since World War II, but many people still farm.

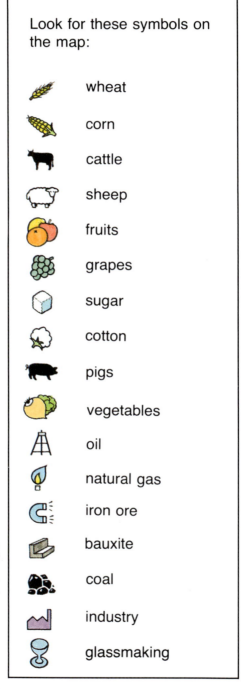

Look for these symbols on the map:

	wheat
	corn
	cattle
	sheep
	fruits
	grapes
	sugar
	cotton
	pigs
	vegetables
	oil
	natural gas
	iron ore
	bauxite
	coal
	industry
	glassmaking

Fuel industry in Romania
Oil lies below the Danube plain of Romania. The oil is pumped up and sent to nearby refineries to be turned into gasoline, chemicals, artificial fibers, and dyes. The main natural gas field is in an area called Transylvania. Long pipelines carry the gas to cities and factories.

Glassmaking in the Czech Republic
Sand from Bohemia is heated with other materials. This forms a liquid that hardens into glass.

Farming in Serbia and Montenegro
Many people in Serbia and Montenegro work on the land, raising sheep, pigs, and cattle. Farmers also grow wheat and corn. Most farms are small.

Coal mining in Poland

Poland is one of the world's leading producers of coal. Some is burned as fuel in factories.

Shipbuilding in Poland

One of Poland's biggest industries is shipbuilding. Many ships are exported. The ships are built in huge covered sheds. Work can go on all through the winter.

Fruit drying in Greece

Grapes have been dried here for hundreds of years. The ripe grapes are picked. Then they are spread on racks in the sun to dry completely before being packed. The small white grapes become sultanas, the small black ones become currants, and the large white ones become raisins.

People and how they live

Most children in Eastern European countries usually start school when they are six years old. After eight years of general study, they may concentrate on a few of the subjects they are particularly good at. If young people show talent in art, music, science, or athletics, they are sometimes encouraged to have special training in these activities during their time at school or college. And there are plenty of opportunities for all children to keep fit. Sports like swimming, basketball, and soccer are popular.

Home for most people in the cities is a crowded flat in an apartment house, which is often shared with grandparents and other members of the family. Country people in Romania live in small wooden houses. They may decorate the walls with colorful woven rugs, painted plates, and wood carvings.

In Poland, most people live in large apartment buildings in the cities.

In Romania, many children join clubs or youth groups. They take part in sports and hobbies and often go on outings. These students are surfing the Internet at school in Bucharest, Romania's capital and largest city.

Every year a huge gymnastics festival is held in Prague in the Czech Republic. Many Czech children perform special exercises at the festival. They spend a long time preparing for the event.

In Greece, people meet at the cafe, drink coffee and other beverages, and share the day's news.

Most people in Albania live in villages and earn their living by working on farms. Market day is an important meeting time for the local people. This outdoor market is in Tiranë, Albania's capital.

All these people live in Eastern Europe.

85

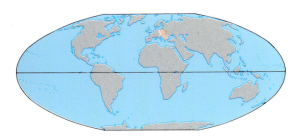

The cities

Warsaw looks like an old city. It has narrow houses, small winding streets, and a market place paved with cobblestones. But all these are fairly new. During World War II, which took place from 1939 to 1945, the center of the city was destroyed by guns and bombs. After the war, the ruins were cleared away and the old town was rebuilt. By looking at old pictures, the architects were able to design houses that looked just like the original ones. Today, Warsaw is a peaceful place with many churches and open-air cafes.

Many other cities in Eastern Europe were badly damaged during the war. Parts of each city now have wide streets and tall blocks of offices but, like Warsaw, they are still proud of their old-style buildings.

⇧
Warsaw is the capital city of Poland. Warsaw has some fine museums and libraries. The huge Palace of Culture and Science is in the modern part of the city.

On a high hill in the center of **Athens,** Greece, is an ancient fortress called the Acropolis. Here stand the ruins of some of the finest and oldest buildings in the world, including the marble Parthenon and other temples. Below the Acropolis is the modern city of Athens.

⇩

Prague is the capital of the Czech Republic. This beautiful city has been called the "Rome of the North." Like Rome, which is in Italy, Prague is built on seven hills and has many historic buildings. Prague is also the center of rail and road routes that link Germany with Poland and Hungary.

→

Budapest, the capital of Hungary, is made up of two cities. Buda is on the west bank of the Danube River, and Pest is on the east bank. The cities united in 1873. Budapest is Hungary's main manufacturing and banking city. Its factories make chemicals, textiles, and transportation equipment.

↓↓

Sofia is the capital and largest city of Bulgaria. The National Assembly meets in this building and chooses Bulgaria's prime minister. The city is famous for its hot mineral spring and for its ancient mosques and churches.

→

Welcome to Russia and its neighbors

Russia and its neighbors cover a vast area. The area is so big that when the sun is rising in the eastern region, the western part has just begun to get dark!

This region spans two continents—Europe and Asia. It stretches from the Baltic and Black seas in the west to the Pacific Ocean in the east. There are many kinds of scenery. In the far north, the land is bitterly cold, with no trees. Father south, a magnificent, dark, evergreen forest called the taiga runs right across the region. And in the far south there are high mountains, deserts, and grasslands called steppes.

Gymnastics are very popular.

Equator

Russian ballet companies are world famous.

Moscow's Red Square is a central meeting place.

46000

In the north, it is cold and snowy for more than half the year.

Many people work on huge farms.

Cars, buses, and trucks are made in Moscow's factories.

The Siberian tiger is the largest tiger in the world.

The countries

In 1991, the Union of Soviet Socialist Republics (U.S.S.R.) ceased to exist. The fifteen republics that made up the U.S.S.R. declared their independence. Most of them joined together to form an association called the Commonwealth of Independent States (CIS). This informal association was made to help give the newly independent republics some economic and military stability during their transition.

Because it has borders with many other countries, this region is in a good position for trading.

The history

For hundreds of years this area was ruled by czars (kings). The czars lived in great luxury and built many beautiful palaces for themselves. But many people were very poor. In 1917, there was a revolution, and the czar was overthrown. Finally, the Communist political party took charge and declared that no one should be rich or poor any more, but that everyone would be equal.

For many years, the U.S.S.R. kept its distance from the rest of the world. The people worked hard to make their country a major world power. They were often suspicious of foreigners. But today, Russia and its neighbors are much more friendly with the rest of the world and want to trade and exchange information on a wide range of subjects.

The Winter Palace, built in the mid-1700's, is now part of the Hermitage Museum in St. Petersburg.

The government

In 1917, the Communist Party took over the government of the country. It was the only party allowed. The central government in Moscow made all the decisions affecting the country as a whole. But in 1990, the

Armenia
Azerbaijan
Belarus
Estonia
Georgia
Kazakhstan
Kyrgyzstan

Latvia
Lithuania
Moldova
Russia
Tajikistan
Turkmenistan

Ukraine
Uzbekistan

Murmansk

Arctic Ocean

Bering Sea

Ob

R U S S I A

Lena

Yakutsk

Sea of Okhotsk

Yekaterinburg

Ob

Yenisey

Angura

Lena

Aldan

Omsk

Novosibirsk

Krasnoyarsk

Lake Baikal

Irkutsk

Sea of Japan (East Sea)

Astana ■

Irtysh

KAZAKHSTAN

Lake Balkhash

Darya

Vladivostok

TAN

Almaty

Bishkek

KYRGYZSTAN

Dushanbe

TAJIKISTAN

country's leaders decided that other parties could be formed. Eventually, the Communist Party lost control. Each republic in the region now has its own government.

Facts about Russia and its neighbors

There are fifteen countries in the region.

Area: 8,600,386 square miles (22,274,896 sq. km).

Population: About 285,549,000.

Largest country: Russia.

Highest mountain: Pik Imeni Ismail Samani, in Tajikistan, is 24,590 feet (7,495 m) high.

Longest river: The Lena is the longest river entirely within Russia. It is 2,734 miles (4,400 km) long. The Volga River is the longest river in the European part of Russia. It is 2,193 miles (3,530 km) long.

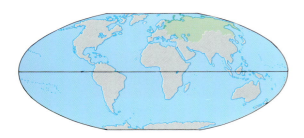

Looking at the land

Ukraine is a huge area of lowland that lies to the north of the Black Sea. In early April, soft breezes warm the flat plains of Ukraine, and the last patches of snow begin to melt. Farmers lead their cattle to the fields and prepare the land for spring planting.

Southeast of Ukraine are the rugged Caucasus Mountains. They form a kind of bridge between the Black Sea and the Caspian Sea, the world's largest inland sea.

High mountains lie between the European Plain and the vast northern region of Siberia. Siberia is mainly a wilderness of plains and highlands and is crossed by some of the world's longest rivers. To the south of the mountains lie snow-capped mountains as well as almost waterless deserts, such as the Karakum.

The **Volga** is the longest river in Europe. It flows into the Caspian Sea. Much of the river freezes for three months every year. Many dams have been built across the river, forming large, man-made lakes.

The dams control the flow of water needed for homes and factories. There are electric power stations at the dams. Ships must go through locks in the dam to move upstream and downstream.

The flat grasslands of the region are called **steppes.** These grasslands are much like the vast prairies of North America, although they are much colder in the winter. The steppes stretch from southern Ukraine into central Asia. The steppes have now been turned into farmland.

Siberia stretches across more than half of Russia. The land is covered by ice and snow for six months of each year. In the north and east of Siberia, the soil under most of the surface remains frozen all year. This frozen layer is known as permafrost.

Ural Mountains

Siberia

steppes

The **Karakum Desert** covers almost all of Turkmenistan, an area east of the Caspian Sea. Here it is hot and very dry. The dry sand is blown into dunes by the wind.

The **Caucasus Mountains** form a huge mountain range that rises between the Black Sea and the Caspian Sea. The range stretches for 752 miles (1,210 km) and is part of the boundary between Europe and Asia. The highest peak in the Caucasus Mountains is Mount Elbrus.

The plants

In winter, cold winds whistle across the flat, barren land of the tundra, the northernmost part of Russia. Here the temperature remains below freezing for eight months of the year. Snow swirls around like fine powder, clinging to the branches of small, bent willow trees. Where the snow has blown away, there are patches of moss and lichen. Here only dwarf trees and shrubs grow, and only the toughest plants can live through the long, cruel winter.

To the south of the tundra, the weather is warmer. Forests of evergreen trees blanket the countryside from east to west. The great steppes, or grasslands, stretch to the south. Parts of the south are dry, stony deserts.

club moss

feather grass

sedge

tulip

anemone

tamarisk

Grassland

In the steppes, or grasslands, the soil is rich, but there are few trees. Many kinds of tough grasses and sedges grow here. In spring, some parts are covered with wildflowers.

Desert

In the desert, the summer days are very hot, but the temperature drops sharply at night and throughout the long winter. The wind carries no rain to these inland areas. Tamarisk trees and shrubs grow where the soil is sandy. But almost nothing grows in the clay soil.

94

bilberry

lichen

arctic willow

wood cranesbill

saxifrage

Tundra

In the area called the tundra, the deep soil below the surface layer of the ground is always frozen. It is hard for plants to grow. In the far north there are only mosses, club moss, lichens, and small shrubs such as arctic willows. Flowers, such as the saxifrage and wood cranesbill, bloom in the summer. Farther south grow dwarf trees, bilberries, and tough grasses.

spiny astragalus

white saxaul

toadstool

alder

Taiga

The taiga is a huge area of forest that stretches across Russia. Most of the trees are conifers, such as pines, larches, firs, and spruce. During the short summer, the topsoil warms and the taiga is like a bog.

pine

larch

Siberian spruce

white birch

95

The animals

polar bear

The dark, cold taiga stretches all the way across Russia. In winter, there is snow in this forest area for several months. The basic winter food of many animals is the seeds of the conifer trees. The great brown bear is one of the taiga's largest animals. It feeds on berries, roots, grubs, and meat.

North of the taiga it becomes too cold for many animals. This is the tundra region. Some animals, such as the reindeer, have adapted to life in the cold. The deer use their wide hoofs to scrape away the snow in search of lichens. South of the taiga, the grassy steppes provide food for grazing animals, such as the saiga antelope. When the snows melt, the snow buntings arrive and feed on the swarms of insects.

Cold coast
Some animals spend most of their time in the icy coastal waters of the tundra region. Polar bears live on the ice floes, and seals and walruses swim in the cold seas.

Siberian tiger

brown bear

lynx

wisent

lebentine viper

Taiga
Huge brown bears live in the forests, feeding on berries and roots and the meat of smaller animals. The lynx, a short-tailed, tufted-eared cat, is another forest hunter. A small number of great bison, called wisents, roam in the far west. The snowy spruce forests of far eastern Russia are the home of Siberian tigers—the biggest tigers in the world.

Desert
There are many kinds of jerboas living in the sandy soil of the desert. They feed at night on shoots and seeds. Lizards, such as the monitor lizard, are common. They feed on insects and small animals. In turn, they are eaten by snakes.

seal

walrus   guillemot

reindeer   wolf

Tundra

Of the animals that live on the
tundra, the largest are wolves
and reindeer. Smaller animals,
such as lemmings, feed on the
shoots of plants and grass. The
tundra is often alive with blood-
sucking mosquitoes, deer flies,
and gnats. Snow buntings nest
here during the warmer months.

lemming   snow
                 bunting

saiga antelope

cobra

marbled polecat

monitor
lizard

Grassland

Bobak marmots live in long,
underground burrows on the flat
steppes. They are hunted by
marbled polecats. Saiga
antelopes live in the drier parts.
Their downward-pointing nostrils
help them to breathe the dusty
air. Young saigas are often prey
for wolves.

jerboa

hamster   bobak
                 marmot

Growing and making

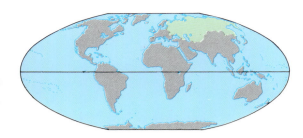

The people of the village were gathered together in a happy crowd. The village had been awarded a special prize. The man from the government told them that the village farm had had the best harvest in the area.

Much of the land used to be divided into big farms called collectives. Each family on the collective had its own plot of land. The government bought the crops at a set price. Factories were run in the same way. But now, the people themselves are taking over the management of farms and factories.

This region has many natural resources, such as coal, iron ore, and nickel. Steel and iron are made to be used in the shipyards and factories. Natural gas and oil are pumped from underground.

Factories

There are many big factories in the region. Some make cars, and others make heavy machinery used on the farms. St. Petersburg is famous for its shipbuilding yards. It is also the largest port in Russia.

Look for these symbols on the map:

- wheat
- corn
- cattle
- sheep
- nickel
- sugar
- cotton
- timber
- fishing
- pigs
- oil
- natural gas
- iron ore
- industry
- coal

Farming

Much of the land in the region is farmed. Wheat, rye, corn, and oats are grown on the steppes. This region is one of the world's leading producers of wheat. In Ukraine, cattle and pigs are raised.

Oil

This region produces a tremendous amount of oil. Many people work on the oil rigs in the Volga-Ural oil field. There are also pockets of natural gas under the ground. A huge pipeline carries the gas to the main cities.

Fishing

Fishing is an important industry. Fishermen catch cod, herring, and salmon in the North Sea and the Pacific Ocean. Sturgeon is caught in the Caspian Sea. Sturgeon eggs, called caviar, are exported all over the world.

Iron ore

In Ukraine, iron ore is mined and melted in huge, hot vats. The melted iron is poured into molds and cooled as ingots, or bars. Much of the iron is made into steel. Iron and steel are needed for shipbuilding and for making machinery.

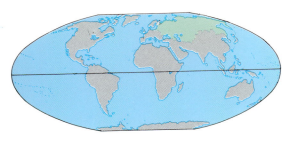

People and how they live

When the Soviet republics became independent, the people were free to return to their own traditional customs and beliefs. Many of the former republics changed the official language from Russian back to their local language.

But the new countries still share many problems. Most of the people live in overcrowded towns and cities. Many families live in apartments with only one or two rooms. Sometimes more than one family share a home. Shopping for food and clothes can be difficult, too. There are often long lines, and some foods are very expensive.

Children attend school from about age six to seventeen. After school, the children take part in club activities such as crafts, music, or sports.

The famous GUM shopping area in Moscow is across Red Square from the government buildings of the Kremlin. Sometimes fruit, vegetables, and meat are in short supply and shopping can be difficult.

Some of the world's best gymnasts have come from Russia and its neighboring countries. Soccer, ice hockey, rowing, and track and field are also popular.

100

All these people live in Russia and its neighboring countries.

In the countryside, many people live in small, wooden houses. These houses often have no gas, electric power, or running water. Most of the people work on huge farms but may also have small plots of land on which they grow their own vegetables. They can then sell these at local markets.

The cities

Like many Russian cities, Moscow is a mixture of the old and the new. Many of the grand, old buildings date back to the days before the Revolution of 1917. Before that time, Russia was ruled by a czar (king). The members of the royal family lived in beautiful palaces and houses in the city. Many elegant theaters, halls, and churches were built at this time. Many of the churches are very old. They are easily recognized by the beautiful decorations on their walls and roofs. Saint Basil's Cathedral stands in Moscow's Red Square. It has colorful onion-shaped domes.

⇧
Kiev is the capital city of Ukraine. The city is an important road and rail junction, and also a busy port. Ships can travel up the Dnieper River from the Black Sea.

⇦ **Moscow** is the capital city of Russia and one of the largest cities in the world. In the center is the Kremlin, which was originally a fortress. It is now the center of Russian government. In Red Square stands the colorful Saint Basil's Cathedral, which is now a museum.

Tashkent, the capital of Uzbekistan, has been an important market and trading place for hundreds of years. Once, caravans passed through, following the famous Silk Road from Europe to China. Today, Tashkent is a modern city. But, in the older part, it still has a traditional marketplace.

There are nearly 700 bridges in St. Petersburg. This beautiful city was built on marshy ground and has many waterways running through it. The largest waterways carry merchant ships from the Volga River to the Baltic Sea. St. Petersburg is famous for its fine buildings.

Novosibirsk was built in the 1890's. It is the largest town in Siberia. Railroads from eastern and western Siberia meet here on the banks of the Ob River. It is also an important center for industry, producing trucks, mining equipment, steel, plastics, and chemicals. Novosibirsk has a university and a large scientific research facility.

On the Trans-Siberian Express

The wheels of the huge engine turn slowly as the long train begins to pull out of the station in Moscow. Excited passengers crowd behind the windows of the coaches and wave to friends and family. Many will ride the train to the end of its journey along the longest railroad in the world. This is the famous Trans-Siberian Express, which begins its journey in Moscow and travels more than 5,592 miles (9,000 km) to Vladivostok, on the shores of the Pacific Ocean.

Once out of Moscow, Russia's main transportation center, the train moves across the European Plain. Most of the people in Russia live here. The soil is rich, and there are many modern industries. The passengers admire the rolling countryside. The journey will take about seven days, and so everyone is relaxed. Many drink tea and talk. The train makes many short stops along the way. The travelers buy cakes, fruit, or hot potatoes from people waiting on the platforms.

The passengers spend time reading or looking out the window at the changing scenery.

Moscow

Nizhny Novgorod

Black Sea

Volga

Ural Mountains

Irtysh

Ob

Lake Baikal

Omsk

Novosibirsk

Caspian Sea

From the European Plain, the track leads into the Ural Mountains. These old, rounded mountains are not very high. They do, however, contain huge deposits of minerals.

Now the railroad passes through large industrial cities such as Omsk and Novosibirsk. These cities depend very much on trains for carrying goods and raw materials.

Ahead is Lake Baikal. It is the deepest freshwater lake in the world.

At one time the train had to cross the lake by ferry to reach the track on the other side. Now the express can run south along the rugged shores of the lake and then east around its tip. This was one of the most difficult stretches of railroad to build.

Some of the passengers have been on board for many days now. They will be glad to reach Vladivostok and the end of their journey.

At last the travelers catch sight of Vladivostok. They will always remember the dramatic landscape, the snowy forests, and the bright blue skies of their long train journey. The Trans-Siberian Express certainly has a special magic.

The Trans-Siberian Express stops at small stations along the way.

Vladivostok

Welcome to Southwest Asia

Southwest Asia is the part of Asia that lies closest to Europe. In fact, a small part of one country, Turkey, is actually in Europe.

Apart from Turkey, this whole region has few people living in it compared with many other parts of the world. The land is often dry, and few crops will grow without irrigation. Most of the people live near the coast where sea winds cool the air and sometimes cause rain.

In the last half of this century, oil fields have been developed in many countries in the region. Some of the countries have become very rich, and their people have taken on new, modern life styles very quickly. But tradition is still important to many people.

Craft workers are important in Southwest Asia. Some of their best-known products are beautiful woven carpets.

The patterns in woven carpets are often very detailed.

Equator

The camel is still a form of transportation in the desert.

Muslims worship in beautifully decorated mosques.

Wandering people, called nomads, live in the Arabian desert region.

Money from selling oil has been spent on modern roads, hospitals, schools, and universities.

Oil is an important export.

The countries

Southwest Asia is made up of 16 countries. Saudi Arabia is the largest, but Iran, Iraq, Turkey, and Afghanistan also cover vast areas.

To the west of this region, across the Red Sea, lies Africa. To the east are China and India. To the north are Europe and Russia and her neighboring states.

The history

Thousands of years ago, great civilizations developed in the valleys of two great rivers, the Tigris and Euphrates. Ruins of cities from that time are still being uncovered in the desert.

All these civilizations were destroyed about 3,000 years ago by a series of powerful conquerors. Finally, Alexander the Great united much of the region, and a rich and powerful empire grew up. In the A.D. 600's, the region was united further by a new religion based on the teaching of the Prophet Muhammad. His followers are called Muslims. For a long while, the Arabs were famous as scholars and skilled builders. Their most beautiful designs were used to create religious buildings called mosques.

In modern times, Great Britain, France, and Turkey have all ruled parts of this region. But most countries had become independent by 1949.

In 1948, the state of Israel was formed so that Jews from around the world could settle there. But this was done against the wishes of the Arab countries. There has been much fighting and unrest between Israel and its Arab neighbors. In 1990, Iraq invaded Kuwait and started the Persian Gulf War. An international force drove Iraq out of Kuwait.

The Omayyad Mosque is in Damascus, the capital of Syria.

The government

Saudi Arabia is a monarchy ruled by a king. The king is the head of the government, as well as the country's religious leader. The royal family has thousands of members. They choose the king from among themselves. A council of ministers helps the king rule.

Some of the other countries are also ruled by kings. Others, like Israel, are democratic republics. This means that people vote in elections to choose members of parliament and a president. The Israeli parliament is called the Knesset.

Afghanistan

Bahrain

Cyprus

Iran

Iraq

Israel

Jordan

Kuwait

Lebanon

Oman

Qatar

Saudi Arabia

Syria

Turkey

United Arab Emirates

Yemen

Facts about Southwest Asia

There are sixteen independent countries in the region.

Area: About 2,642,288 square miles (6,845,306 sq. km).

Population: About 284,509,000.

Largest country: Saudi Arabia.

Highest mountain: Mount Nowshak on Afghanistan's border with Pakistan is 24,557 feet (7,485 m) high.

Longest river: The Euphrates River, which flows from Turkey through Syria into Iraq, is about 1,700 miles (2,736 km) long.

Black Sea

■ Ankara

TURKEY

Caspian Sea

CYPRUS

Mediterranean Sea

■ Tehran

Kabul ■

SYRIA

AFGHANISTAN

Beirut ■

LEBANON ■ Damascus

Euphrates

Tigris

■ Baghdad

IRAN

Jerusalem

Gaza Strip

■ West Bank

IRAQ

Dead Sea

ISRAEL

JORDAN

KUWAIT

BAHRAIN

Persian Gulf

Riyadh ■

QATAR

UNITED ARAB EMIRATES

Muscat ■

Red Sea

SAUDI ARABIA

OMAN

● Mecca

Sanaa

■

YEMEN

The wealth

For thousands of years, farmers have grown crops on the fertile plains near the coast and along the banks of the rivers. In the open spaces of the desert that covers most of Southwest Asia, wandering herders look after their sheep as they have always done. But oil has been discovered under the desert and the sea, and now there are many oil wells. These have brought wealth to many countries that used to be poor.

109

Looking at the land

Hot desert covers much of Southwest Asia. All day, the strong sun beats down on the empty land. Only lizards come out in the scorching heat, which may reach as high as 122° F. (50° C). The rocks expand with the heat of the sun during the day. But as the orange sun sets, the desert becomes very cold. And at the end of the day, the rocks cool and shrink. This makes them crack and split apart. This is one way in which the desert landscape is always changing. Even the shifting sand makes sure that the scenery never stays the same. Winds carve out new shapes in the sand dunes, and sometimes shift huge amounts of sand from one place to another in a whirling sandstorm.

As well as deserts, there are also wet mountain areas in Southwest Asia, especially in the north. Some long rivers start in these mountains and flow across the desert to the sea.

Mount Ararat is the highest mountain in Turkey. It is 16,946 feet (5,165 m) high. Snow covers the mountain in winter. In spring, the snow melts and feeds the rivers.

The **Dead Sea** is really a large saltwater lake. The shores are about 1,300 feet (400 m) below the level of the nearby Mediterranean Sea. This is the lowest point on land anywhere in the world. The hot sun dries up the shallow waters, leaving salt caked on rocks and dead trees.

The **Red Sea** has this name because the water really does sometimes turn red. It is colored by tiny algae plants that grow there in the summer.

The **Euphrates** is the longest river in Southwest Asia. It starts high in the mountains of Turkey. The river has cut deep valleys through the land.

Winding roads zigzag through the mountain passes of the **Hindu Kush,** a huge mountain range in central Afghanistan. It has several of the world's highest peaks.

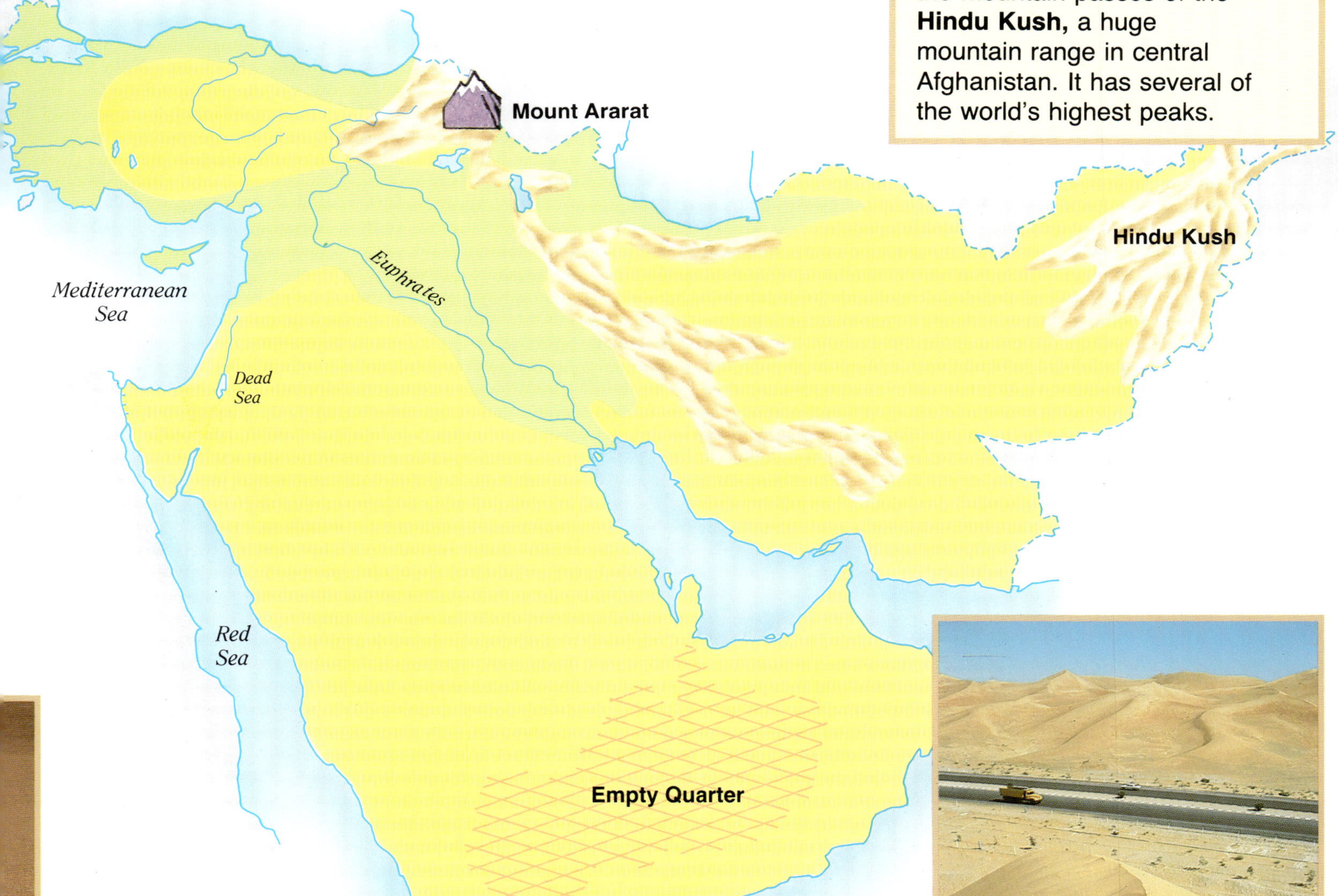

Mount Ararat

Hindu Kush

Mediterranean Sea

Euphrates

Dead Sea

Red Sea

Empty Quarter

Most of the Arabian Peninsula is a dry wilderness. In the south lies one of the world's driest places. It is called the **Empty Quarter** because so few people live there. Sand dunes cover much of the land.

Plants and animals

The dry river bed, or wadi, stretches for many miles (kilometers) across the rocky plateau. Heavy rain may fall for only a few hours each year. Then this dusty channel becomes a raging torrent, carrying boulders along with it. When this rushing water has disappeared, a few pools remain. Animals come to drink at the pools until this water dries up, too. Noisy flocks of birds crowd around the water. Hoopoes call as they fly down from the ridges above, where scrub warblers are nesting. Whenever a dark shape glides overhead, the birds of the wadi freeze and fall silent. The sharp-eyed lanner falcon will swoop down on anything that moves.

Many of the countries of Southwest Asia are hot and dry, with huge sandy deserts. But, in places, a few broad rivers flow through green valleys. There are some large lakes where pelicans and other water birds live. Black bears live in the high mountain forests on the east, among tall trees of cedar, spruce, and pine.

Lake

At the lakesides, the Egyptian mongoose searches for water-birds and their eggs in the reeds. The jungle cat prowls the reed beds, too, hunting for frogs and voles. White pelicans make a curved line around a shoal of fish and drive them toward the shore. In the shallows they can easily scoop up the fish in their huge beaks.

Fertile valley

The green valleys are dotted with tall date palms. Long-legged buzzards perch in the trees. The rollers catch insects in flight. In an Acacia bush, a sunbird uses its long bill to find nectar and insects in the flowers.

Wadi

After a rain, water collects in the wadi in small pools. Birds, such as the hoopoe and the scrub warbler, come here to drink. The rare houbara bustard fluffs out its feathers in a mating dance.

kingfisher

papyrus

Egyptian mongoose

jungle cat

spruce

cedar

High forest

Spruce, pine, and cedars grow in the mountain forests. The Asian black bear looks for ants, grubs, and berries. The beech marten hunts for small birds and their eggs. The ratel, or honey badger, prefers the honey from wild bees' nests. The Afghan pika lives in rocky places. It stores hay in a burrow for the winter.

beech marten

Asian black bear

pine

ratel

Afghan pika

Arabian oryx

Nubian ibex

glasswort

tamarisk

golden jackal

striped hyena

Desert

The rare Arabian oryx is well-adapted to life in the desert. It gets the water it needs by eating plant roots. The Nubian ibex hops nimbly from rock to rock. It feeds on the leaves of tamarisks and glasswort. These plants store water during dry periods. The striped hyena hunts grazing animals.

113

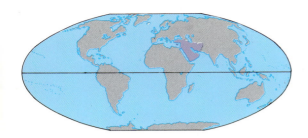

Growing and making

Clouds of hot, dry sand swirl across the desert. Sand dunes stretch as far as the eye can see. At first, this looks like a land where nothing can live. But here and there, clusters of healthy trees and green plants break the bare landscape. Rows of bushes are covered with juicy fruit, which will soon be ready for picking. All that is needed to make the desert bloom is fresh water. Desert places that have fresh water are called oases. In other areas, the water has to be brought to the desert in pipes. This water is mainly seawater from which the salt has been removed.

Part of the money earned from selling oil and gas has been used to help farmers and create new industries in the Arab countries. They have been able to buy seeds and machinery and pay for irrigation and land improvements. Apart from oil, fruit growing is important to the countries of Southwest Asia. People also work in traditional industries, such as carpet weaving and rug making.

Irrigation in Southwest Asia
Many desert areas have been made fertile by bringing water to them. This is called irrigation.

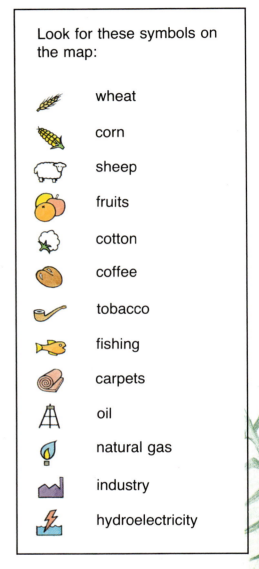

Look for these symbols on the map:

	wheat
	corn
	sheep
	fruits
	cotton
	coffee
	tobacco
	fishing
	carpets
	oil
	natural gas
	industry
	hydroelectricity

Date growing in Oman
One of the main exports from Oman is dates. The date palms grow in oases along the northern coast. The fruit hangs in clusters of up to 1,000 dates. The dates are picked and their stones removed. The fruit is then washed and dried in the sun or in special ovens. The dried dates are pressed into small blocks and packed.

Oil in Saudi Arabia

Saudi Arabia is one of the world's leading exporters of oil and oil products. There are over forty oil fields, mostly in the east of the country, on the coast. The chief oil field of Ghawar is the largest oil field in the world. Saudi Arabia also has large amounts of natural gas.

Carpet weaving in Turkey

Handmade rugs and carpets are woven on tall looms. They have rich patterns and take a long time to weave.

Citrus fruits in Israel

Israel grows large amounts of citrus fruit such as oranges, grapefruit, lemons, limes, and tangerines. Much of the fruit is sold through special government markets. All Israeli fruit is stamped *Jaffa*. Jaffa is the name of one of the oldest cities in the world. Today it is part of the busy, modern city of Tel Aviv-Jaffa.

115

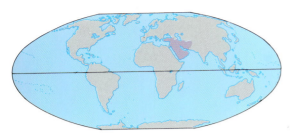

People and cities

Well over 200 million people live in Southwest Asia, and many of these are Muslims, who practice the religion of Islam. In Southwest Asia there are great religious centers where Muslim, Christian, and Jewish pilgrims go to pray or seek a special blessing. An important Muslim center is the city of Mecca, in Saudi Arabia. Here, there is a huge cube-shaped building called the Kaaba, where there is a black stone that is believed to have come from Paradise. Each year, hundreds of thousands of pilgrims worship at the Kaaba during a special pilgrimage called the Hajj. All Muslims must try to visit Mecca at least once in their lifetime if they are able.

Although new ideas are changing the traditional ways of living, most Muslims follow the rules of their religion.

Modern and traditional forms of transportation meet in Saudi Arabia.

Baghdad is the ancient capital of the Arab Empire. It is famous for its fine mosques with their towers called minarets. The mosques are beautifully decorated. They have words from the Koran, the sacred book of the Muslims, written on them.

Mecca is the holy city of Islam. The prophet Muhammad was born here. All over the world, Muslims pray and bow to Mecca five times a day.

A group of people called Pushtuns live in Afghanistan. Most Pushtuns live high up in the mountains.

116

All these people live in Southwest Asia.

Jerusalem is a holy city to the Jews, Christians, and Muslims. The old part of the city holds buildings that are important to all these religions. One of these buildings is the Dome of the Rock, which stands near the wall surrounding the Old City. Narrow streets wind through this section of Jerusalem. But new buildings have been built in the rest of the city.

Welcome to the Indian subcontinent

India, the largest country in the Indian subcontinent, is bordered by the sea, except on the north. Here is the Himalaya, the highest mountain range in the world. India's northern neighbors, Bhutan, Nepal, and China, share these mountainous regions. India's other neighbors are islands in the Indian Ocean, especially the large island at its tip, Sri Lanka.

In Pakistan, farming is successful on the fertile plain of the Indus River. Bangladesh is also a mainly flat farming country. The seasons are usually very hot and dry or very hot and wet.

There are many large cities and towns throughout India where more and more new factories are being built. But traditional customs play a large part in modern everyday life, especially in the countryside.

The leaves of the tea plant are often picked by hand.

Equator

Both the Pakistani and Indian cricket teams have fans worldwide.

The beautiful Taj Mahal was built by an emperor as a tomb for his wife.

The Himalaya forms a high land barrier in the north.

Indian elephants are trained to move heavy loads.

A busy network of railroads crisscrosses the region.

Fine cotton is woven and printed with bright colors.

119

The countries

This region is made up of a group of seven countries. These are Bangladesh, Bhutan, India, the Maldives, Nepal, Pakistan, and Sri Lanka. To the northwest of this area is Afghanistan. To the northeast is China. India is by far the largest country in this region.

For much of the year the climate is very hot. Often there is not enough rain to make crops grow and then people may not have enough to eat.

India has the second largest population of any country in the world. Many people are poor, but most children can have free education. Most villages have electricity.

The history of India

At times in the past, India was made up of several kingdoms. At other times, much of it was ruled as one empire. For much of its history, India was a wealthy region that traded spices, silk, and precious stones with Europe.

From the middle 1700's, Britain gradually took control of much of the Indian subcontinent. But, in the early 1900's, many people in India demanded independence. At this time, many Indian people followed a man called Mohandas Gandhi. Gandhi believed independence could be won by peaceful means. He was right. India was granted independence in 1947.

At the same time two Muslim parts of India broke away to form a new country called Pakistan. Later, East Pakistan became a third country. It is called Bangladesh.

Mohandas Gandhi was an important leader of the Indian independence movement.

The government of India

India is a republic. The head of the government is the prime minister. The prime minister and parliament are elected by the people. In India, everyone over the age of twenty-one is allowed to vote.

The Indian government is trying to help the poor by improving working conditions, making wages fair, and helping the elderly. The government is worried about the size of the population. It is asking people to have small families. If the population continues to grow at the current rate, there may never be enough jobs or land for everyone.

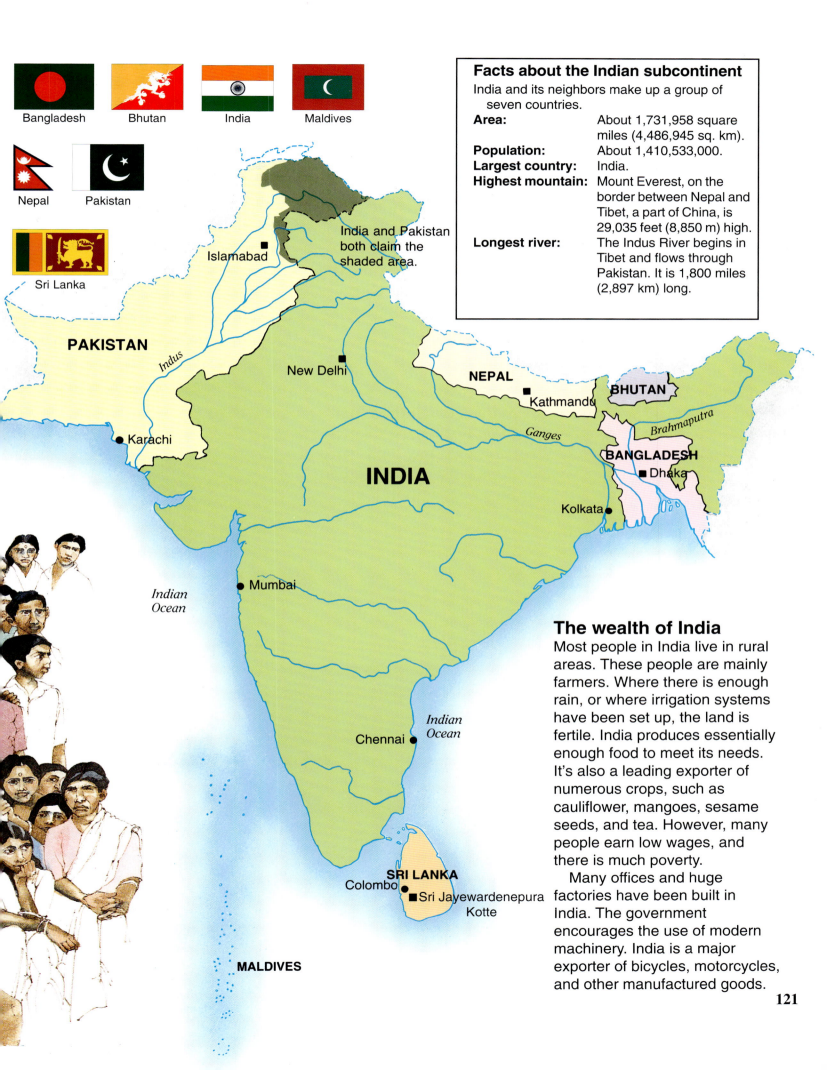

Bangladesh

Bhutan

India

Maldives

Nepal

Pakistan

Sri Lanka

Facts about the Indian subcontinent
India and its neighbors make up a group of seven countries.

Area:	About 1,731,958 square miles (4,486,945 sq. km).
Population:	About 1,410,533,000.
Largest country:	India.
Highest mountain:	Mount Everest, on the border between Nepal and Tibet, a part of China, is 29,035 feet (8,850 m) high.
Longest river:	The Indus River begins in Tibet and flows through Pakistan. It is 1,800 miles (2,897 km) long.

Islamabad

India and Pakistan both claim the shaded area.

PAKISTAN

Indus

New Delhi

NEPAL

Kathmandu

BHUTAN

Ganges

Brahmaputra

BANGLADESH

Dhaka

Karachi

INDIA

Kolkata

Indian Ocean

Mumbai

Indian Ocean

Chennai

SRI LANKA

Colombo

Sri Jayewardenepura Kotte

MALDIVES

The wealth of India
Most people in India live in rural areas. These people are mainly farmers. Where there is enough rain, or where irrigation systems have been set up, the land is fertile. India produces essentially enough food to meet its needs. It's also a leading exporter of numerous crops, such as cauliflower, mangoes, sesame seeds, and tea. However, many people earn low wages, and there is much poverty.

Many offices and huge factories have been built in India. The government encourages the use of modern machinery. India is a major exporter of bicycles, motorcycles, and other manufactured goods.

Looking at the land

On the north side of the Indian subcontinent is the highest mountain system in the world. The melting snows on the Himalaya form rivers that have cut deep valleys in the mountainsides. The rivers flow down into the plains of northern India, Pakistan, and Bangladesh. One great river, the Indus, flows through Pakistan, while the Ganges flows through India into Bangladesh, where it joins the Brahmaputra.

The flat delta of the Ganges and Brahmaputra rivers is a maze of channels and flooded fields. Here and there, houses perch on small patches of dry land. Every summer, the monsoon winds that blow over India bring rains that fill the rivers, causing them to flood and overflow their banks.

The Deccan, a huge plateau, forms most of the southern part, or peninsula, of India. Off the eastern tip of the peninsula is the beautiful island of Sri Lanka, while the Maldives lies to the southwest.

The **Indus** River begins in the mountains of Tibet and flows southward through Pakistan. It crosses deserts and dry grasslands before reaching wide plains. Here irrigation channels help water a vast area of land, making it fertile.

The **Maldives** is a country consisting of about 1,200 small coral islands. Around the coasts are white sandy beaches. Only about 200 of the islands have people living on them.

122

Mount Everest is the world's highest mountain. It is part of the Himalaya, which forms a border between northern India and Tibet. Its peak is 29,035 feet (8,850 m) high.

Himalaya

Indus

Thar Desert

Mount Everest

Ganges

Brahmaputra

Bay of Bengal

Deccan Plateau

A great Indian desert, called the **Thar,** stretches across the northwestern part of India. The land is made up of rocky hills and sand dunes. It hardly ever rains here, but now people have started to irrigate parts of the desert.

Sri Lanka

Maldives

The **Ganges** River flows down from the Himalaya. Before it reaches the sea, it divides into several branches. One branch is joined by a long river, the Brahmaputra. The rivers flow into the Bay of Bengal.

The plants

sweet
flag

The snowy mountain peaks of the Himalaya can be seen through the forest branches. In the foothills of Nepal, tall deodar cedar trees reach toward the sky. Beneath them, rhododendron trees grow. Nearby, on the open slopes, are purple Nepal cowslips and other brightly colored flowers. The warm sun lights up the deep blue of the Himalayan delphiniums.

Below the foothills are the warmer fertile valleys of the Indus and the Ganges rivers. Here, reeds and rushes line the banks. Southward are the drier grasslands of the Deccan, with some trees. To the west, the land is covered with thick forests of timber trees.

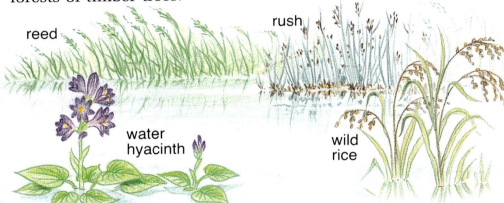

reed

rush

water
hyacinth

wild
rice

Waterside

The Indus and Ganges rivers flow through the northern plains. On some banks, rushes, reeds, and wild rice grow. Sweet flag spreads into shallow waters. Water hyacinths keep the water clean by absorbing many chemicals.

silk-cotton tree

teak

satinwood

ironwood

Western forest

There are thick forests in the west of India. Teak and silk-cotton trees grow here. The hairy seeds of the silk-cotton provide kapok used to fill cushions. Apart from teak, there are many other valuable trees, such as ironwood and satinwood.

124

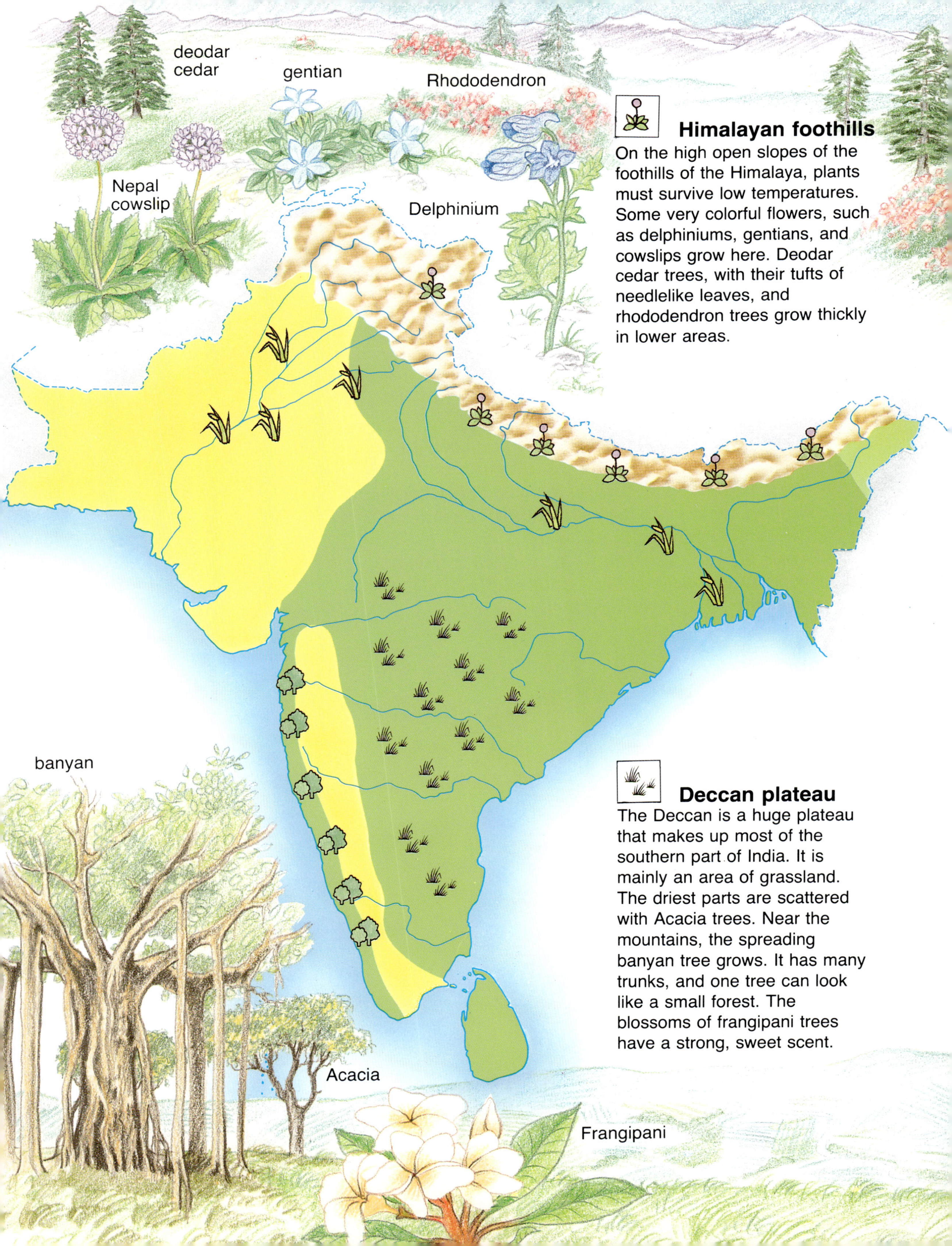

deodar
cedar

gentian

Rhododendron

Nepal
cowslip

Delphinium

Himalayan foothills

On the high open slopes of the foothills of the Himalaya, plants must survive low temperatures. Some very colorful flowers, such as delphiniums, gentians, and cowslips grow here. Deodar cedar trees, with their tufts of needlelike leaves, and rhododendron trees grow thickly in lower areas.

banyan

Deccan plateau

The Deccan is a huge plateau that makes up most of the southern part of India. It is mainly an area of grassland. The driest parts are scattered with Acacia trees. Near the mountains, the spreading banyan tree grows. It has many trunks, and one tree can look like a small forest. The blossoms of frangipani trees have a strong, sweet scent.

Acacia

Frangipani

The animals

hornbill

elephant

axis deer

rhinoceros

Some of the largest animals live in the hill forests of the northeast. The rare Indian tiger spends most of the day asleep in the shade or lying in water to keep cool. Elephants move about the forests, feeding on plants and leaves. In the wetter, swampy parts, the one-horned Indian rhinoceros wallows in mud and grazes on water plants. Many of the smaller forest animals have patterned coats that blend in with the foliage and help them stay hidden.

In the Himalaya, animals must be good climbers to survive. Most have thick, shaggy coats for protection from the cold. To the south is the Deccan plateau, an area of dry grassland. Many kinds of snakes live here. One of their enemies is a fierce little animal called a mongoose.

Sri Lanka, off India's southern tip, is warm and wet. Brightly colored birds and many kinds of climbing animals, such as the loris, live in the forests.

Hill forest
The Indian elephant pulls leaves from the trees with its trunk. It is smaller than the African elephant. Both the large Indian rhino and the tiger are rare animals. Tigers hunt smaller animals, such as the axis deer. These spotted deer can hide well in the forest.

tahr

lammergeier

goral

markhor

hangul

porcupine

mongoose

The Himalaya
Kashmir stags, called hanguls, gaze on the Himalayan pastures. On steeper slopes wild goats, called markhors, and nimble gorals forage for grass. At dawn and dusk the red panda searches for bamboo shoots, roots, and sometimes mice and insects.

red panda

Deccan plateau
Food is scarce on the dry Deccan plain. The gray mongoose eats almost anything. It will fight the deadly cobra, and it usually wins. Vultures are scavengers. They feed on the dead carcasses of animals. Black vultures feed first, followed by the white-backed vultures.

126

desert fox

nilgai

desert cat

blackbuck

see-see partridge

long-eared hedgehog

Thar Desert
Blue bulls, called nilgai, and blackbucks live on the edge of the desert. At night the long-eared hedgehog hunts for insects, lizards, and birds' eggs. The see-see partridge nests here, too. It is hunted by the desert cat and the desert fox.

tiger

flying fox

wild boar

Egyptian vulture

cobra

egret

Sri Lanka
Sri Lanka has many interesting nighttime feeders. The sloth bear feeds on bees and termites, and the pangolin uses its sticky tongue to trap ants. The slender loris catches insects in the trees. The flying fox is a bat. It feeds on fruit.

black vulture

jungle fowl

parakeet

pangolin

slender loris

white-backed vulture

sloth bear

127

Growing and making

Lines of men and women move through the neat rows of tea plants. On their backs, they carry large baskets held by straps across their foreheads. They move quickly through the bushes, picking off young shoots called flushes. Each flush has several leaves and a bud. When the baskets are full, they are weighed and the tea pluckers are paid for each basket they have picked. India grows more tea than any other country, although there are large tea plantations in Bangladesh and Sri Lanka. Other important crops are rice, cotton, jute, sugar-cane, rubber, and coconuts.

Mining is important in both Pakistan and India. Iron ore is mined and used in iron and steel smelting to make heavy metal products.

Look for these symbols on the map:

	wheat
	rice
	cattle
	sugar
	cotton
	tea
	rubber
	coconuts
	peanuts
	timber
	fishing
	industry
	iron ore
	copper
	coal

Tea picking
Tea leaves are picked by hand. They are sorted and dried before they are packed for use.

Farming
Many people on the subcontinent are farmers. Whole families work on the land. Some farmers have tractors and other machines, but most use simple tools. Bullocks are used as work animals. Many areas depend on irrigation for enough water to grow crops. Poor farmers struggle to grow enough food.

Iron and steel production

Since 1950 India has built up its industries from almost nothing. There are now several large iron and steel factories. Iron and steel are used for making train engines, railroad cars, automobiles, and motor scooters.

Rice

Rice is one of the main crops grown in the region. Many people in India and its neighboring countries eat rice as their main food, usually mixed with a few vegetables. The rice is planted by hand in shallow watery beds called rice fields. After about six months, the rice is ready to be picked by hand.

Cotton production

Cotton is an important crop, especially in Pakistan. The white, fluffy bolls of cotton were once picked by hand. Today, they are usually harvested by machine. The cotton fibers are separated from the seeds and cleaned before being combed into long strips and spun into thread.

129

People and how they live

Although the region is fast becoming very modern with large cities and new industries, many people still live and dress in traditional ways. In most parts of India, clothing is loose-fitting, so that people can feel comfortable in the heat. In the mountainous northern regions, such as Kashmir, people wear warmer wool clothes in winter.

Many people live in villages in rural areas. Most make a living by working on the land. Houses often have mud floors, with no running water or electricity. But new cities are growing fast, and many people are leaving the rural areas to work in the cities.

Most Indian people are Hindus, and religion plays a very important part in their lives. The people of Pakistan and many other parts of the subcontinent are Muslims. All over the region religious processions are held throughout the year.

Most Indian food is cooked with spices. Brass cooking pots are set over fires, or in small ovens in the courtyard. Flat bread is baked on a hot metal plate. It is eaten while it is still warm.

Cows are a common sight in Hindu areas, even in the towns. They are allowed to wander until they are collected by their owners at milking time. Hindus never kill cows for food. In the Hindu religion, cows are sacred.

Many women wear earrings, nose ornaments, and brightly colored bangles. Some paint a dot, or a bindi, of colored powder on their foreheads. They choose a powder color to match their dress or sari.

Music is an important part of life on the subcontinent. Traditional instruments include drums and horns and a many-stringed instrument called a sitar. Wedding processions in the Himalaya are often led by musicians.

Elephants have been used in India for centuries to move heavy loads. They are also used in processions, where they wear brightly colored decorations. The passenger box on the elephant's back is called a howdah.

All these people live on the Indian subcontinent.

The cities

The cities of the region are very crowded. Some families are wealthy and live in comfortable houses, but many live in crowded slums. Here, whole families often live together in one small room. Some people have no houses at all and live, eat, and sleep in the street.

People from the surrounding rural areas come to the cities to sell their animals and crops in the busy outdoor markets. The streets are full of color, bustle, and noise all day long. Car horns hoot and bicycle bells ring, while market traders display their goods to passers-by.

Some streets are lined with craft workers' shops. Here, beautiful ornaments of brass, copper, silver, and gold are made and sold. Perfume and expensive spices are on sale, too. All day long, people push their way through the streets, buying and selling.

⇑

Kolkata is one of the most overcrowded cities in the world. Disease and hunger are common in the slums, which are known as bustees. But there are also many fine houses in the center of Kolkata. Nearby, there is a large park, the Maidan, where cows graze and cricket is played.

⇐ **New Delhi** is the capital city of India. It is about 3 miles (5 km) from Delhi, the old capital city. New Delhi has plenty of space. There are wide, treelined streets and modern buildings. The city has some huge government buildings, such as the Parliament House and the Secretariat.

↑

Islamabad is the capital city of Pakistan. The city was built in the 1960's. Before then, Karachi was the capital. The name Islamabad means "City of Islam." The government of Pakistan meets in a modern building in the city.

Mumbai is one of the busiest seaports in the world. Near the harbor stands a huge arch which is known as the "Gateway of India." Mumbai, an important center of industry, has factories that make dock and railroad equipment and cotton mills.

↓

↑

Over four million people live in **Chennai,** India's fifth largest city. Workers cycle to their jobs at the large factories where automobiles and railroad cars are made. There are also cotton mills and leather tanneries, and ships from all over the world use the busy harbor.

In the foothills of the Himalaya

Once, Himalayan explorers and Everest mountaineers had to make the long walk from Kathmandu to the lower slopes of the Everest chain of mountains. Today, a short flight in a small plane brings them into the tiny airstrip of Lukla. Here, the hikers are greeted by their guides. Everyone is looking forward to the journey ahead. In a short while, the party sets off toward the high peaks.

The first part of the track leads the hikers up the valley of the Dudh Kosi River. This river is a tumbling mass of water that has drained from the lower slopes of Mount Everest. The snow that falls above the snow line hardly ever melts, and the rocky peaks that rise above the clouds are always bare. As the group climbs higher, the land becomes rocky.

Crossing and recrossing the river on flimsy bridges, the path zigzags up toward the Khumbu Glacier. The air is frosty here. Looking back, mist is swirling over the river valley. Ahead, the dark pyramid of Mount Everest's peak glows in the setting sun.

Only a few hardy junipers and birch trees survive here. Their trunks are covered with moss and twisted by the wind.

The Himalaya forms a barrier that separates northern India from the plateau of Tibet, in China.

134

Soon the hikers reach the village of Namche Bazar where they share a meal with a local family. Then they snuggle under warm rugs of yak wool for the night.

The next day they reach the last human outpost, an ancient monastery perched high in the mountains. Here the air is low in oxygen, and breathing becomes difficult. But the views are superb. Gigantic mountain peaks—in some parts snowy, in others just bare rock—stand out against a background of bright blue sky.

Thyangboche Monastery stands against the dramatic landscape of the Himalaya. Buddhist priests, called lamas, live behind its white walls.

For this party of hikers, their visit to the slopes of Mount Everest is enough. They won't attempt to climb the great mountain itself. The hikers remember the names of Mount Everest's first conquerors, Tenzing Norgay and Edmund Hillary, and understand the courage and skill it must have taken to reach the mountain's top. Thinking of these two men, the hikers begin to make their way back to Kathmandu to follow other trails through the foothills of the Himalaya.

The Himalaya contains the greatest mountains on earth. Yet life here can be cruel and terrifying. Avalanches of snow can cover small villages on the higher slopes, and rivers often swell and flood the narrow valleys. Earthquakes and landslides change the scenery. The climate is often wet and cold. Sometimes hailstones fall—some so big they bruise the skin—and strong winds destroy tiny mud-brick homes.

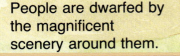

People are dwarfed by the magnificent scenery around them.

Hikers in the Himalayan foothills see all these things. But, like the local villagers who worship the great mountains, they can only wonder at the size and beauty of the towering peaks.

Welcome to China and Eastern Asia

China is the largest country that is completely in Asia. And it is the third largest country in the world.

China stretches from central Asia to the Pacific Ocean—across almost 3,000 miles (4,828 km) of mountains, desert, and fertile plains. In the southeast, it is very hot and rainy for much of the year. This is the region where most of China's crops are grown. It is also where most of the Chinese people live. In much of the north, the land is dry and bare, with bitterly cold winds.

More people live in China than in any other country. About one of every five people in the world lives there. The Chinese call their official language putonghua, which means "common language." Instead of an alphabet, Chinese writing uses a system of word signs, called characters.

This is the Chinese way of writing *welcome.*

Most of the Chinese people work on the land.

Equator

There are many street markets in Hong Kong.

The giant panda lives in central China.

China's Great Wall is about 4,500 miles (7,240 km) long.

The Imperial Palace stands in Beijing.

Southeastern China is one of the most beautiful parts of the country.

Silkworms are used to make silk.

137

The countries

This region is made up of China, Mongolia, North Korea, South Korea, and Taiwan. Across the northern borders are Russia and its neighbors. The Indian subcontinent is in the west, and Burma, Laos, and Vietnam lie to the south.

China is the largest country in the region. It is surrounded by bleak deserts, great mountain ranges, and seas. For many hundreds of years, these natural boundaries acted as barriers. They kept China separate from the rest of the world.

The history of China

The Chinese empire began more than 2,000 years ago. The history of that time, the thoughts and traditions of its people, were written down. They are still read today.

Under their rulers, the Chinese built great cities and created splendid works of art. It was in China that paper, the compass, porcelain china, and gunpowder were invented. The ancient Chinese were great astronomers and doctors.

The Chinese empire lasted until the 1900's, when revolution and war broke out. Today, China is taking a growing part in world affairs.

The government of China

Almost all the members of China's government belong to the Chinese Communist Party. About 1 in every 20 people is a member of the Communist Party, and anyone who wants an important job must join.

Party members are chosen to represent villages and towns, and they in turn choose representatives for their region. The most important members of the party serve on the Central Committee. Many Chinese would like to see their government become more democratic.

In early times, fearsome statues were made to guard the entrances of palaces and temples.

Facts about China and Eastern Asia

There are five countries in the region.

Area: 4,398,479 square miles (11,396,254 sq. km).
Population: About 1,415,639,000.
Largest country: China.
Highest mountain: Mount Everest, on China's border with Nepal, is 29,035 feet (8,850 m) high.
Longest river: The Yangtze, in China, which is 3,915 miles (6,300 km) long.

China   Mongolia   North Korea

South Korea   Taiwan

MONGOLIA
■ Ulaanbaatar

Amur

NORTH KOREA
■ Pyongyang

Beijing ■

■ Seoul

SOUTH KOREA

Yellow Sea

CHINA

Huang He

Huang He

Mekong

Yangtze

Brahmaputra

● Lhasa

Yangtze

Shanghai ●

■ Taipei

TAIWAN

Xi Jiang

Macao ● ● Hong Kong

The wealth of China

The government plays a big part in all the important industries and everything to do with trade and money. Outside the cities, peasant groups and families farm the land for themselves. Although China is a huge land, and more than half of its people are farmers, there is barely enough food for everyone. Only a small part of the land can be cultivated.

The Chinese government is worried about the high population. It tells people not to get married until they are over 25 and to have small families.

The government wants to make China a richer and more modern country. It has encouraged new industries to start. It has improved schools and hospitals. It has also told the Chinese people to work especially hard in industry and farming.

139

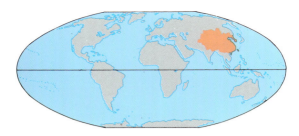

Looking at the land

Earthquakes are common in northeastern China. They sometimes do a lot of damage. Chinese scientists tour the region, hunting for signs that might mean an earthquake could occur. They use an instrument called a seismograph that measures movement in the earth's crust. In 1975, scientists were able to warn people that there would be an earthquake in the city of Haicheng. Just two hours after the people had been led to safety, the city was destroyed.

Flooding is also a problem in China. The Huang He River flows through the wide plain of northern China. This river used to flood every few years, damaging villages and crops. Now, high man-made riverbanks and dams have been built to help stop the flooding.

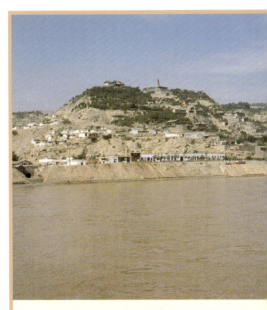

The name **Huang He** means "Yellow River." It is yellow because it carries so much fine, yellow-colored soil. The Huang He flows into the Yellow Sea.

North of the Himalaya mountain system is the plateau of **Tibet.** This is the world's largest and highest plateau. Much of Tibet is a wasteland. The soil is frozen for most of the year. But on some slopes, the land has been cut into terraces. When the snows melt, water is trapped on the terraces and rice is grown.

The **Yangtze** is one of the longest rivers in the world. It begins high up in the mountains and flows quickly through steep, rocky gorges. Near the sea, the river widens and is busy with boat traffic.

The **Gobi Desert** lies partly in northern China and partly in Mongolia. The desert is made up of sandy soil and rocky plains. There are also areas of dry grassland. Unlike many deserts, the Gobi is bitterly cold in winter. In the summer months, the region becomes very hot for long periods of time. The Gobi is a very dry place and only a few trees can grow there.

Gobi Desert

Tibetan Plateau

Huang He

Huang He

Yellow Sea

Yangtze

Yangtze

Miraculous Pinnacles

The **Miraculous Pinnacles** are some of the most unusual features of China's countryside. They are steep, limestone hills, and they rise almost straight up from the ground. There are only small areas of flat land between them.

141

The plants

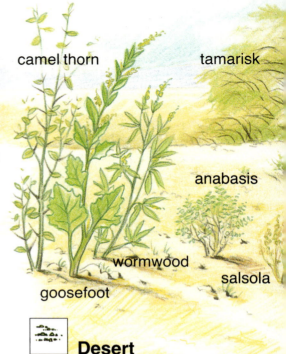

camel thorn

tamarisk

anabasis

wormwood

salsola

goosefoot

By early summer, the thick snows have melted, and China's high forest region is a mass of color. The ice has vanished from the banks of the streams, and wild rhododendrons, with their white, red, pink, and purple flowers, cover the slopes. The dark trunks of fir and spruce trees tower above these colorful shrubs, and maple and birch trees carry new leaves. Giant stems of bamboo rustle in the breeze.

On the Tibetan plateau, the plants are very different. Only small flowers and grasses can grow here, where it is so cold. In the desert region of Mongolia, rain hardly ever falls, so there are few plants. The northern plains are covered with grasses, herbs, and some small trees.

Desert

The rocky Gobi Desert is dry and cold. Few plants grow here. The roots of the tamarisk spread a long way to find moisture, and goosefoot survives even in the driest parts. Camel thorn is very prickly. Only the tough-mouthed camel can eat its stems.

iris

anemone

lacquer tree

blue poppy

Himalayan edelweiss

handkerchief tree

cinnamon

rhododendron

Tibetan plateau

In the high mountains of Tibet, flowering plants must fight the cold. Some, such as edelweiss, have fluffy leaves to protect them from the wind. Many flowers with bright colors, such as blue poppies and gentians, attract insects. Lacquer trees grow on the lower slopes.

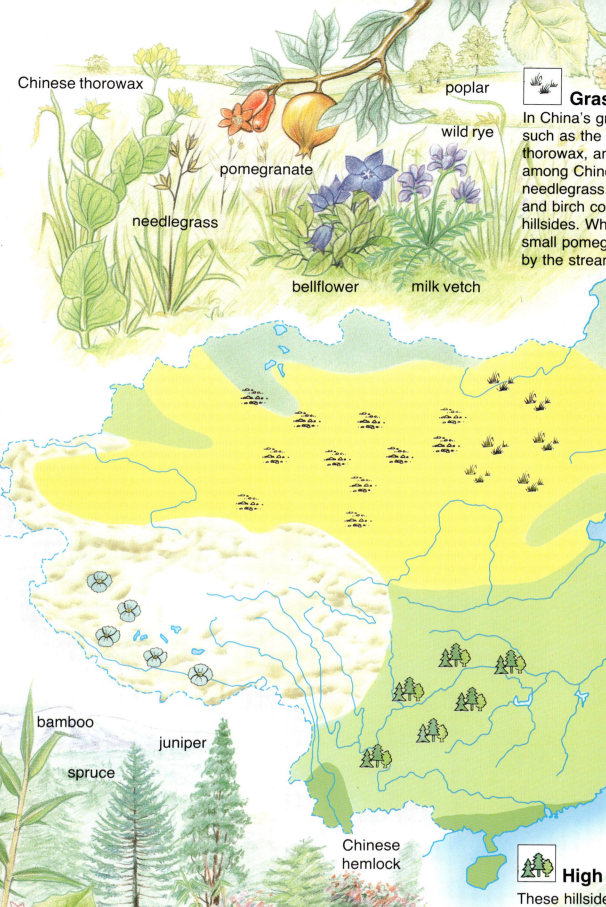

Chinese thorowax

pomegranate

poplar

wild rye

white mulberry

needlegrass

bellflower

milk vetch

Grassland

In China's grasslands, herbs such as the milk vetch, Chinese thorowax, and bellflower grow among Chinese wild rye and needlegrass. Forests of poplar and birch cover some of the hillsides. White mulberry and small pomegranate trees grow by the streams and rivers.

bamboo

juniper

spruce

Chinese hemlock

Azalea

Chinese vine

High forests

These hillsides are wet and warm in summer and cold and snowy in winter. Several types of bamboo grow here. Some kinds flower only once in sixty years. Colorful azaleas grow beside rhododendrons, junipers, and cinnamon trees.

143

The animals

Przewalski's horse

Bactrian camel

Mongolian gazelle

tiger weasel

corsac

five-toed jerboa

gecko

There are great forests of bamboo in the Sichuan region of central China. This area is the home of the black and white giant panda, which feeds mainly on bamboo. It bends and tears down the tall bamboo stems, and then crunches the young shoots and leaves. Other animals live in the forest, too. Brightly colored pheasants roost in the low bushes, and bamboo rats burrow for roots in the soft earth. Overhead, golden monkeys run along the branches from tree to tree.

To the west of the Sichuan region, on the high plateau of Tibet, live animals well suited to the cold. Some, such as the yak, have thick undercoats to protect them from the bitter winds.

Some kinds of water birds make their homes by the lakes and rice fields near the Yangtze River. The cold, dry Gobi Desert was once home to herds of wild horses. And it is one of the few places in the world where camels still roam free.

Desert

Two-humped Bactrian camels live in China's dry regions. They have long coats to protect them during the cold winters. Tiger weasels and foxes, called corsacs, are the nighttime hunters of this region. They hunt smaller animals, such as geckos and jerboas.

Tibetan plateau

Only the strongest animals can survive in these cold uplands. Yaks are well protected by their thick, shaggy coats. Chiru and gorals graze here beside wild blue sheep. They are hunted by the pale-coated snow leopard and large birds of prey.

Himalayan griffon

black vulture

snow leopard

yak

chiru

goral

blue sheep

Sichuan Mountains

Bamboo is the main food of the black and white giant panda and the takin. Colorful pheasants live in the mountain forests, and golden monkeys leap through the trees. The fire-tailed sunbird feeds on insects and nectar from the flowers.

golden snub-nosed monkey

takin

monal pheasant

sunbird

bamboo rat

144

Steppe

Great bustards stalk the grasslands in search of insects. Pikas, ground squirrels, and dwarf hamsters feed on the grasses. They are hunted by upland buzzards and tawny eagles. Pallas' cat, and snakes, such as Haly's pit-viper, also hunt here.

Haly's pit-viper

great bustard

upland buzzard

pika

Pallas' cat

ground squirrel

dwarf hamster

golden pheasant

giant panda

white-breasted kingfisher

Chinese water deer

Wetlands

The white-breasted kingfisher, the fish owl, and the Chinese pond heron fish in the lakes and rice fields of the east. The Chinese water deer lives here, too, feeding on water plants.

brown fish owl

Chinese pond heron

Growing and making

Inside the silk factory there is great noise and bustle. Everyone is very busy. The silk has been spun, dyed, and wound on large reels. Now these are stacked in banks of bright color. A worker lifts reels onto a conveyor belt to be taken off for packing. The silk will be sent all over the world to be woven into cloth. The Chinese have made silk for thousands of years. Merchants from Europe used to travel to China along a special road called the Silk Road just to buy it.

China still makes more silk than any other country. Farming is also very important in China, and many crops and animals are raised to feed the country's large population. Great wealth can also be found under the ground. China and some of its neighbors mine for minerals, such as coal, iron ore, gold, and oil. Much of the mining equipment is old, and work is slow. Another important industry is the making of electrical appliances, such as radios and television sets. These are produced in China, Taiwan, and South Korea.

Silk making in China

The silk moth lays eggs that hatch into silkworms. Chinese workers feed them mulberry leaves. After several weeks, the silkworms spin cocoons around themselves. The cocoons are taken to factories where the silk is picked off and spun into threads.

Look for these symbols on the map:

- wheat
- rice
- corn
- wool
- cotton
- tea
- tobacco
- timber
- fishing
- pigs
- oil
- iron ore
- gold
- coal
- industry
- silk
- tungsten

Mining in China

Mining is very important in China. Under the ground, there is iron ore, coal, gold, and a metal called tungsten. China produces more tungsten than any other country.

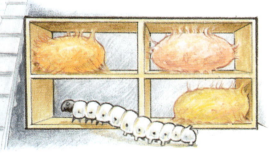

Chemical industry in China

Chinese farmers use large amounts of fertilizer to help their crops grow. Factories make fertilizer from chemicals. The farmers also use as much natural manure as possible. This manure comes from animal dung and human waste.

Herding in Mongolia

In southwest Mongolia there are flat, grassy plains called steppes. The soil here is too poor for growing crops. Instead, herdsmen raise cattle, sheep, and horses. Wool, meat, and animal skins come from Mongolia.

Farming in China

More than half the people in China work on the land. There is very little modern machinery. The farmers use simple tools and have oxen to pull their plows and carts.

Industry in Hong Kong

Hong Kong produces many radios. More than half of Hong Kong's workers are in manufacturing industries.

People and how they live

Cooking and eating well are considered to be very important in China. The Chinese understand that certain foods help to keep people healthy, and most Chinese eat only food that is absolutely fresh. Today, Chinese food is famous throughout the world. Certain foods are considered to be treats, such as bird's nest or sharkfin soup, sea cucumbers served with lotus roots, and water chestnuts.

But for most Chinese people, food, clothing, and homes are simple. Clothing is designed to be both useful and comfortable. Many people wear loose-fitting trousers and jackets in plain colors. About two-thirds of the people live in rural areas in China, in villages and small towns.

The Chinese celebrate the beginning of their New Year with a parade. A team of people is needed to wear this giant dragon costume made of silk and velvet. The dragon dances along the street, followed by people beating drums and clashing cymbals. The crowd enjoys the fireworks displays.

All these people live in China and Eastern Asia.

Chinese food is cut into "bite-sized" pieces, cooked, and then eaten with chopsticks.

Many Mongols live in traditional tents called yurts. A yurt has a circular frame made of light wood. Sheets of felt are draped over the frame and covered with grease to keep out the rain and cold. Inside the yurt, a cooking fire is lit in the middle of the floor.

In China musicians play traditional and modern instruments. The two-stringed violin is a traditional instrument. It is played with a bow. Music usually accompanies all plays performed in China.

Chinese children begin school when they are six or seven years old. They need to learn between 3,000 and 5,000 Chinese "characters," or word signs. And so, learning to read and write is hard work.

Many Chinese fishermen use wooden sailing boats called junks. After each fishing trip, they unload their catch and then return to sea. Some families live on board the junks. Life is cramped, but the families sleep on deck when the weather is warm.

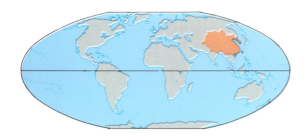

The cities

There are few cars in China, so most people in the cities go to work by bicycle. In Beijing alone, there are millions of bicycles! The roads are also crowded with buses, handcarts, and pedicabs—tricycles with carriers for people or goods. The streets are very noisy, too. Horns hoot and toot and bicycle bells jingle. Policemen stand on platforms to direct the traffic and keep it moving. They carry loudspeakers to shout warnings at people. Anyone who ignores a red light will be stopped and fined. The rider may even have the bicycle taken away.

China's cities and towns are busy and crowded. About seven million people live in the capital, Beijing. And bustling Shanghai is one of the biggest cities in the world. City homes are often in modern apartments that are sometimes shared by two families.

Beijing has been the capital of China for more than 1,000 years. It has most of the government buildings and more than thirty universities, colleges, and technical schools. In the center of Beijing is the huge Tiananmen Square, one of the largest city squares in the world. Next to this is the Forbidden City, which was once the home of the Chinese emperors.
⇩

Seoul, the capital of South Korea, was badly damaged during the Korean War (1950-1953). But much of the city has been rebuilt. It has also grown quickly, as people from rural areas flocked in to find work. Seoul is South Korea's major industrial city.

Lhasa is one of the most remote cities in the world. It is the capital of Tibet, and a trading center for furs, tea, wool, and salt. Lhasa has many Buddhist temples. Its most famous building is the huge Potala. This was once a palace of the Tibetan religious leader, the Dalai Lama. ⇐

The name **Hong Kong** means "fragrant harbor." More than five million people live in Hong Kong, on China's southeast coast. Hong Kong's natural harbor helps make it an important center for world trade and industry. ⇓

Shanghai is the most crowded city in China. About thirteen million people live in the city and its suburbs. The city is the center of the country's industry and the most important seaport. Factories in Shanghai produce cotton and silk cloth, iron and steel, and oceangoing ships. ⇓

Along the Great Wall

The bus leaves Beijing in the morning to travel 25 miles (40 km) to the Great Wall.

On the way, the guide tells the history of the wall, explaining how separate sections were started, probably in the 400's B.C. to keep fighting tribes apart. This massive task was ordered by the first emperor of China, Shi Huangdi. The guide tells how the parts were later joined into one long wall. It took many hundreds of years to complete. The guide traces the zigzag route of the Great Wall across a map of China. The passengers in the bus marvel that a wall could stretch on and on for about 4,000 miles (6,400 km).

Watchtowers stand all along the wall. Each was manned by a soldier who kept watch for enemies attacking from the north.

Jiayuguan

Gobi Desert

Huang He

152

The passengers get out of the bus in a large square. There are a few sheds in the square where souvenirs are on sale.

Everyone climbs a stairway to the tall gateway that marks the beginning of this part of the Great Wall. The top of the wall is a wide roadway, wide enough for five horses to gallop beside each other. From the gateway, the line of the road snakes away uphill and disappears into the far distance. For the first mile, the roadway climbs upward in steps. A great stone watchtower rises above the parapets. A second and third tower rise farther on. Towers like these stand at regular intervals all along the wall.

Some people have explored the whole length of the wall. They have traveled westward from Dandong, following the line of mountains to the north of Beijing. Here the wall has recently been restored. But in many places, where the stones have been ripped down over the years to build houses and other buildings, only crumbling ruins remain. Sometimes as ruins, sometimes as high battlements, the wall twists on through the mountain passes, skirting the southern edge of the Gobi Desert. Finally, after thousands of miles, the wall comes to an end in the sandy desert near the city of Jiayuguan.

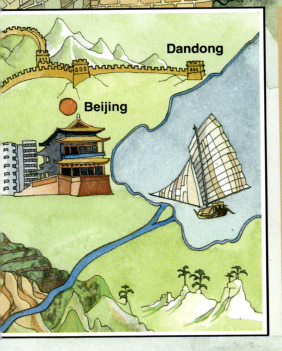

Dandong

Beijing

The Great Wall of China stretches for about 4,000 miles (6,400 km).

153

Welcome to Japan

Japan is an island country in the North Pacific Ocean, just off the coast of mainland Asia. Most people live on the island of Honshu, where many large cities have been built.

Japan has cold, snowy winters and cool summers. The southern islands are warmer than the others. Most of Japan's coastline is rocky. Inland, it is very mountainous, with few flat areas. There are many volcanoes, and earthquakes are common.

Japan is one of the most industrialized countries in the world. Electronic products and cars are produced and exported all over the world. Japan's cities house millions of people. When the streets fill with workers during the daily rush hours, traffic almost comes to a stop.

Fish is an important food in Japan.

Flower arranging is a traditional art.

Equator

Japan has many Buddhist temples.

A traditional Japanese house is very simple.

154

Japan makes many electronic products.

The volcano Mount Fuji is one of Japan's most beautiful sights.

Paper kites are flown at special festivals.

Tokyo is the capital city of Japan.

The country and the land

Japan is a land of many islands. There are four main ones—Honshu, Hokkaido, Kyushu, and Shikoku—and thousands of smaller ones. The islands form a curve about 1,200 miles (1,900 km) long. In the southwest, Japan is about 480 miles (800 km) from China. In the north, Japan is less than 180 miles (300 km) from Russia.

The Japanese islands are part of a range of high volcanic mountains. The most famous peak in Japan, Mount Fuji, or Fujiyama, is an inactive volcano that last erupted in 1707. Jagged mountain peaks, thick forests, rushing rivers, thundering waterfalls, and quiet lakes make Japan a land of great natural beauty.

Facts about Japan

Japan consists of four major islands—Honshu, Hokkaido, Kyushu, and Shikoku—and thousands of smaller ones.
Area: 145,870 square miles (377,801 sq. km).
Population: About 127,638,000.
Largest island: Honshu.
Highest mountain: Mount Fuji, on Honshu, is 12,388 feet (3,776 m) above sea level.
Longest river: Shinano River, on Honshu, is 220 miles (367 km) long.

The history

For much of its early history, Japan was a troubled nation. Strong families and generals called shoguns fought for control. For more than a thousand years, the emperor had no real power and ruled in name only.

In the early 1600's, Japan's rulers cut the country off from the rest of the world. They believed this would help keep order within the country.

In 1868, the emperor regained his traditional powers. Many Western ideas were introduced, and foreign trade was encouraged.

Beginning in the 1930's, the Japanese conquered much of Eastern Asia. Although defeated in World War II, Japan has become a great industrial power.

Many Japanese Buddhists visit the Great Buddha statue. Buddhism came to Japan from China and Korea about A.D. 552.

The wealth

Since the 1950's, Japan has become the strongest economic power in Asia. High-quality manufactured products, ranging from tiny computer chips to huge oil tankers, are made in Japan's modern factories. These items are exported to almost every country in the world. Japan also manufactures many products in other countries.

The government

Japan's head of state is the emperor. The country's laws are made by the Diet, an elected body of legislators. The day-to-day government is conducted by the prime minister and his Cabinet.

Hokkaido is a beautiful island of forested hills and mountains. Many people visit Hokkaido to enjoy its natural parks. Heavy snowfalls during the long winters make this a good place for winter sports. **Lake Shikotsu** is in the Shikotsu-Toya National Park. The lake formed as water collected in the crater of an extinct volcano.

The northern part of the island of **Honshu** is very mountainous, but there are areas of level land. Some of the level land is flooded for paddy fields in which rice is grown. Other crops are also grown. Farther south is the Kanto Plain, the largest area of level land in Japan.

Japan

Mount Fuji, or Fujiyama, is Japan's highest peak. It is an inactive volcano.

Sea of Okhotsk

Hokkaido

• Sapporo

Lake Shikotsu

JAPAN

Honshu

Shinano

Sea of Japan (East Sea)

Japanese Alps

Kanto Plain

Tokyo ■
• Yokohama
Kamakura

Mount Fuji

• Nagoya

Kyoto •

• Osaka

Pacific Ocean

Shikoku

Kyushu

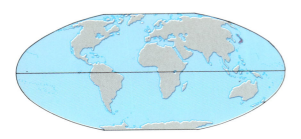

Plants and animals

sea lion

sea eagle

spotted seal

The mountain ranges of Honshu stand above neat rice paddies and terraces. The mountain slopes are covered with a thick forest of birch trees. This area is rich in wildlife. It is the home of a noisy but timid monkey—the Japanese macaque. Macaques travel about the forest in large groups. Japanese macaques often sit in hot pools to keep warm! Another unusual forest creature is the serow. It is an antelopelike goat and lives only in Japan. In winter, serows feed on tree shoots in the forests. In summer, they journey to graze in the high meadows.

Japan has many wonderful wildlife habitats. The northern island of Hokkaido is different from other parts of Japan. It has high mountains where snow falls for nearly half the year. Here, huge brown bears hunt for mice under the tree roots and Japanese cranes make lively courtship displays. In the south, it is much warmer. Around these shores, there are dolphins and many kinds of fish.

Cold coast

Groups of spotted seals live off Japan's northern coast. Huge sea lions live here, too. The males have thick manes of fur around their necks. Sea eagles swoop down to catch fish from the cold waters.

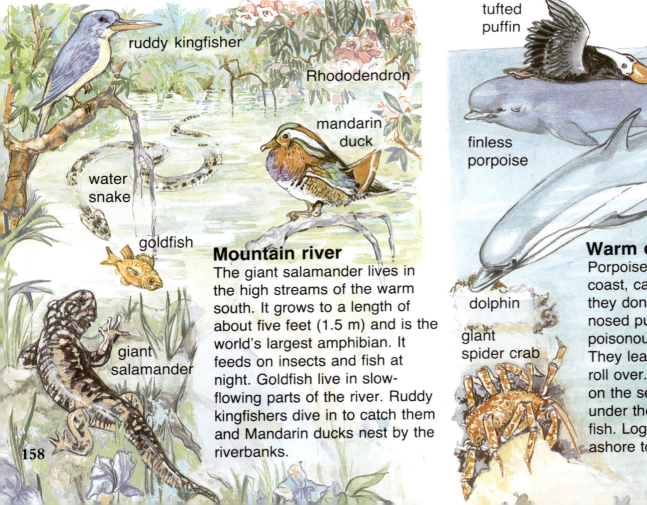

ruddy kingfisher

Rhododendron

mandarin duck

water snake

goldfish

giant salamander

tufted puffin

finless porpoise

dolphin

giant spider crab

puffer fish

Mountain river

The giant salamander lives in the high streams of the warm south. It grows to a length of about five feet (1.5 m) and is the world's largest amphibian. It feeds on insects and fish at night. Goldfish live in slow-flowing parts of the river. Ruddy kingfishers dive in to catch them and Mandarin ducks nest by the riverbanks.

Warm coast

Porpoises swim around the coast, catching small fish. But they don't touch the sharp-nosed puffer fish because it is poisonous. Dolphins like to play. They leap out of the water and roll over. Giant spider crabs live on the sea bottom. Puffins swim under the water, scooping up fish. Loggerhead turtles come ashore to lay eggs.

Hokkaido

Japanese cedar

Junipers, tall spruce trees, and Japanese cedars cover the mountain slopes. The large brown bear roots for mice in the forests. In spring, the Siberian rubythroat arrives, and Japanese cranes court each other with singing and dancing.

brown bear

spruce

Siberian rubythroat

arolla pine

Japanese crane

Japanese macaque

birch

juniper

hare

Dall's porpoise

serow

sika deer

loggerhead turtle

raccoon dog

fox

Honshu

In the northern forests of birch and pine, the raccoon dog feeds on insects, fruit, and small animals. Japanese macaques and sika deer are shy forest animals, and so is the serow. It eats herbs and the shoots of young trees.

159

Growing and making

The Japanese factory is the scene of bustle, noise, and movement as the conveyor belt carrying a line of car bodies moves by. Each time the line stops moving, large robot-controlled spot welders move in on both sides. They look like giant birds. The car panels are welded into place, and the line moves on again.

Japan produces more than eight million cars a year. It is one of the top car-producing countries. Japanese cars are sold all over the world and are famous for their high quality.

In addition to cars, Japan also exports ships and electronic equipment. Fishing and timber are also important industries in Japan. Japanese workers are very loyal to their companies and almost never change their jobs. Many workers spend their free time together. They even go on company vacations.

Look for these symbols on the map:

	wheat
	rice
	cattle
	dairy products
	fruits
	tea
	timber
	fishing
	vegetables
	pigs
	coal
	industry
	ship-building
	car manufacturing
	computers
	TV sets

Car manufacturing

Car manufacturing is important in Japan. The cars are sold to people in many countries all around the world.

Forestry

Most of Japan's uninhabited areas are covered by forests. Trees grow quickly here because there is plenty of sun and warm rain brought by the summer monsoons. Many trees are used in papermaking. The forests are a part of Japan's natural beauty.

160

Electronics

Japan makes and exports huge numbers of electronic and electrical appliances, such as television sets, radios, cassette players, and home computers. Japan is the world's leading maker of television sets. Many parts for these products are made in Japan but are put together and finished in other Asian countries where workers are paid less. As a result, Japanese products can be sold at lower prices.

Fishing

The Japanese fishing fleet ranges from small ships that stay near the coast to large, deep-sea trawlers. The main fish caught are tuna, sharks, salmon, and sardines. Squid are also caught. In Japan, many fish are raised on fish farms. The Japanese eat more fish than meat.

Shipbuilding

Japan has been the world's leading shipbuilder for many years. Many of the big oil supertankers are built in Japan. These huge ships are used to carry oil from Southwest Asia. Japan has to import most of its oil and iron ore, yet it is still a leading world producer of steel.

161

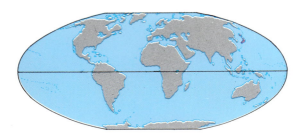

People and cities

Japan is one of the most crowded countries in the world. Most of its huge population lives near the coast, especially in the four main cities, Tokyo, Yokohama, Osaka, and Nagoya. Concrete and steel office buildings tower upward in these busy cities, and many people live in tall apartment buildings.

Japanese families enjoy the peace and calm of a garden. Because there is very little space in the cities for parks or gardens, the people make small gardens wherever there is a patch of land. This love of nature comes from Japan's major religion, Shinto. Followers of Shinto believe that gods are found in mountains, trees, and other natural things. Many Japanese also follow the Buddhist religion. They try to lead a peaceful and happy life through goodness and wisdom. In modern Japan, these two ancient religions are important in everyday life.

↑ In Japan, grandparents help care for children. Japanese children go to school five and a half days a week. They learn to read and write the Japanese language, which is made up of word signs called characters.

All these people live in Japan.

↑ On special days, girls wear the traditional kimono, a long silk robe fastened around the waist with a sash called an obi.

Each year a festival of ice sculpture is held in **Sapporo,** the capital of Hokkaido. Some sculptures look as though they are made of glass, but in fact they are carved from ice. Sapporo is a ski resort in winter.

The city of **Kyoto** was founded more than a thousand years ago. The city has many beautiful Buddhist temples and shrines.

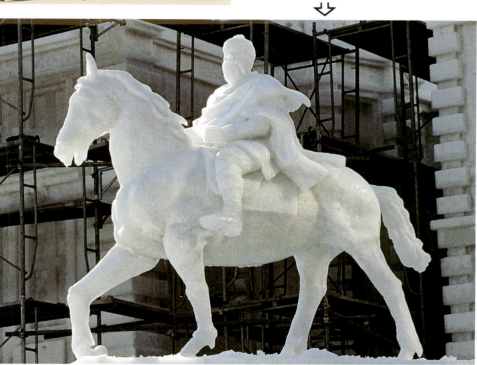

Most Japanese people live in cities. **Tokyo** is the capital city. Its busy streets are lined with huge modern office and apartment buildings. On clear days, people in Tokyo have a spectacular view of Mount Fuji, Japan's highest and most famous peak.

163

Welcome to Southeast Asia

Southeast Asia is made up of several countries, many of which are islands or groups of islands. Indonesia is the world's largest island group. This country is made up of more than 13,600 separate islands that spread out over about 3,000 miles (4,800 km) of ocean. Many of the islands are covered with tropical forest, because this area of the world is always hot and wet. The equator runs through the center of the region. Moist winds bring heavy downpours throughout the wet monsoon season each year.

Many of the islands are volcanoes, and the lava from them has created rich soil. Bamboo grows here, as do some valuable timber trees, such as teak and mahogany.

Equator

Hillsides are terraced to make paddy fields for growing rice.

Bangkok is famous for its temples and palaces.

The juice of the rubber tree is made into the bouncy kind of rubber we know.

Orangutans and hornbills live in the mountain forests.

There are many volcanoes in Indonesia and the Philippines.

In Thailand, fruit and vegetables are sold from boats at floating river markets.

Singapore is a small, modern island country.

165

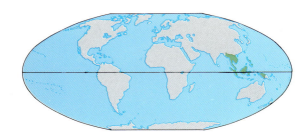

The countries

There are eleven countries in Southeast Asia. They are Brunei, Cambodia, East Timor, Indonesia, Laos, Malaysia, Myanmar (also called Burma), the Philippines, Singapore, Thailand, and Vietnam. Some of these countries are large groups of islands.

To the west of Myanmar and Laos is India. To the northeast of the region is China. To the southeast, the region's nearest neighbors are Papua New Guinea and Australia.

Many of the countries of Southeast Asia are surrounded by sea. The people have developed skills in making many things for their own needs. Today their products are shipped all over the world.

The history

More than a thousand years ago, the people of this region grew wealthy through trade with China and the Arab lands. They created many splendid works of art. From the 1500's on, European sailors explored the region. These explorers also claimed parts of the area for their own countries. These areas became colonies that were ruled for a long time by France, Britain, the Netherlands, Portugal, and Spain.

Only Thailand remained independent. For more than 200 years members of the Thai royal family have ruled the country.

As time went by, all the colonized lands of Southeast Asia wanted to be independent and rule themselves. Some became independent peacefully. In other areas, there was fierce fighting that went on for years. There was also civil war in some countries, such as Vietnam and Cambodia. This brought much suffering to the people of these lands.

The wealth

This region is rich in natural resources of many kinds. There are also many rivers and plenty of rain. This, together with volcanic ash, makes the soil rich and fertile. Although the farming methods used in most countries are traditional and slow, many crops are grown and exported. There are minerals and fuel deposits under the ground, but not enough money or machinery to mine them. The forests of Southeast Asia supply most of the world's teak. Fishing is also a major industry.

Most people live and work in rural areas. But small factories have been built where products such as tools, clothing, and household goods are made. In Thailand, Indonesia, Malaysia, and especially Singapore, there are many of these factories. There are also larger factories that manufacture cars and airplane parts.

The rulers of Thailand used to travel in elaborate barges. Today the barges are used on special occasions.

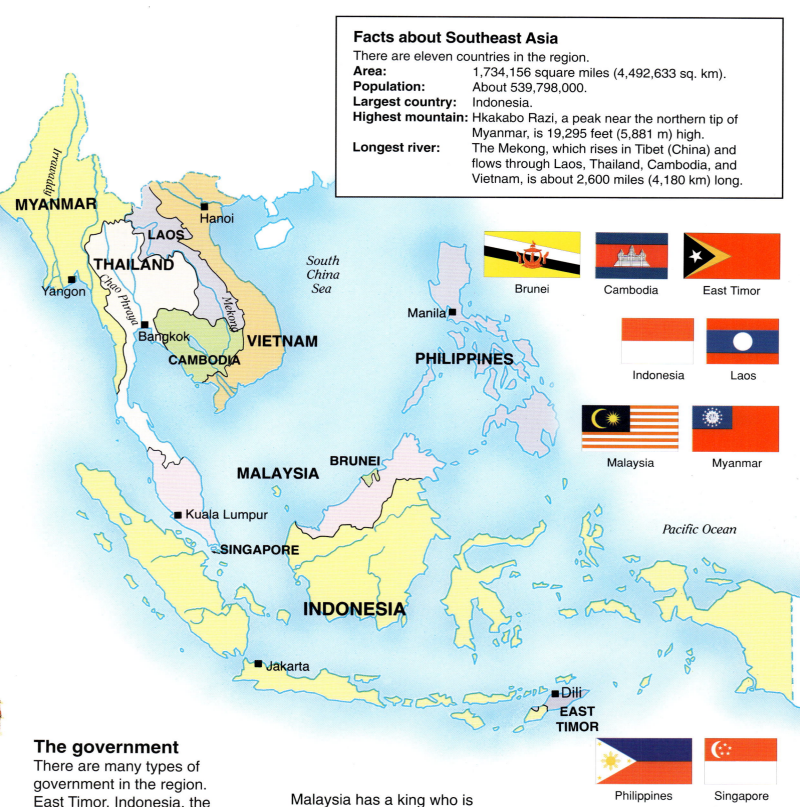

There are eleven countries in the region.
Area: 1,734,156 square miles (4,492,633 sq. km).
Population: About 539,798,000.
Largest country: Indonesia.
Highest mountain: Hkakabo Razi, a peak near the northern tip of Myanmar, is 19,295 feet (5,881 m) high.
Longest river: The Mekong, which rises in Tibet (China) and flows through Laos, Thailand, Cambodia, and Vietnam, is about 2,600 miles (4,180 km) long.

Brunei   Cambodia   East Timor

Indonesia   Laos

Malaysia   Myanmar

Philippines   Singapore

Thailand   Vietnam

The government

There are many types of government in the region. East Timor, Indonesia, the Philippines, and Singapore are republics. They each have several political parties that compete in elections. Myanmar is ruled by a military group.

Brunei, Malaysia, and Thailand are monarchies. Brunei is ruled by a king called a sultan.

Malaysia has a king who is chosen to be the head of state for a short time. But Malaysia and Thailand are really each ruled by a prime minister and parliament, elected by the people. Cambodia, Laos, and Vietnam are ruled by Communist governments.

167

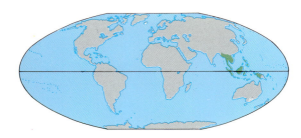

Looking at the land

As farmers work in the flooded rice fields on the island of Java, they keep a watchful eye on the nearby volcano. The smoke they see rising from it is made of steam, gases, and small pieces of hot ash. The farmers know that the mountain is one of the world's most active volcanoes. It has erupted many times in the last 150 years. Each time, it causes great damage. But this time, the scientists will warn them if danger threatens.

Many of the islands of Southeast Asia, including many in Indonesia and the Philippines, started as volcanoes that erupted and pushed up from the seabed. The shape of this region is still changing and growing.

On the wide, flat plains of Thailand, water from the Chao Phraya River is channeled into canals. The canals provide water for the rice fields. Rivers are also important waterways. Many boats transport products along the river.

The Mekong River starts as a fast-flowing stream in Tibet. It flows through five countries. Near the sea, it winds slowly across a large, swampy delta. At the end of summer, after heavy rains, the Mekong overflows. Large areas of land are flooded.

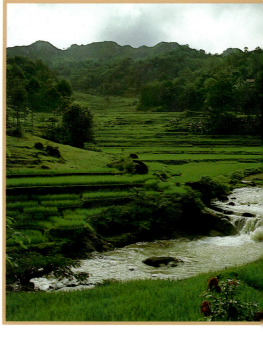

There are more than 7,000 islands in the Philippines. Most of them lie on the edge of a moving piece of the earth's crust. For this reason, earthquakes and volcanoes are common. **Mayon volcano** on the island of Luzon is an active volcano.

Chao Phraya

Mekong

Mayon volcano

Philippines

Chocolate Hills

Indonesia

Java

Indonesia is made up of more than 13,600 islands. Some are very small. Most of the larger islands have volcanoes, and many are still active.

In some places, the sides of the river valleys have been cut into terraces so rice can be grown.

Bohol is an island in the Philippines. It is famous for its hundreds of rounded hills known as the **Chocolate Hills.** The grass on these hills dries out in the hot summer heat and turns a chocolate brown color.

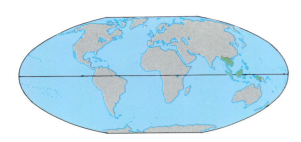

The plants

There's a bad smell hanging in the damp air of the rain forest. Swarms of flies are buzzing over a huge flower on the forest floor. Its bumpy, dark-red petals spread a yard (meter) across, and from its cuplike center comes a smell like rotting meat. It is rafflesia, the largest flower in the world. This plant has no leaves. It gets its food from another plant, a creeping vine. Ginger plants grow nearby, with pepper vines trailing over them. Their red berries are spicy peppercorns. The thick trunks of weeping fig trees rise high above the ground. Their leaves shut out much of the light.

Over 25,000 different flowering plants grow in the rain forests of Southeast Asia—more than in any other single area of the world. The mountain and riverside forests in this region are also filled with wild fruits and flowers.

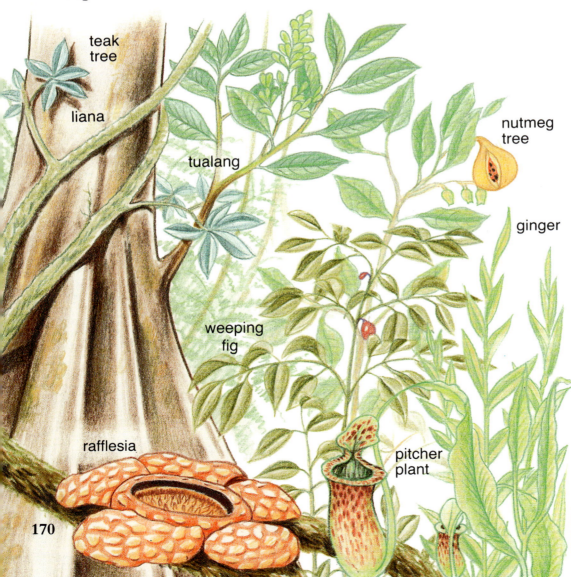

teak tree

liana

tualang

nutmeg tree

weeping fig

ginger

rafflesia

pitcher plant

betel palm

fern

slipper orchid

Riverside forest
Graceful ferns hang from the branches of trees. Betel palms produce nuts that some people chew. Some kinds of wild bananas are very colorful. Below them grow beautiful slipper orchids, which are shaped to attract bees.

Rain forest
The honeycombs of wild bees hang from the branches of tualang trees, which can grow some 260 feet (80 m) tall. Below them grow small nutmeg trees with round, spicy fruits.

Lianas and weeping figs grow among the trees. Pitcher plants trap insects in their pot-shaped leaves.

High forest
On the high mountain slopes, twisted oaks and dwarf trees are covered with soggy mosses. Lichens and orchids grow on the branches. Bamboo and thorny palms cover the ground.

oak

palm

bamboo

Dendrobium orchid

lichen

moss

Mangrove swamp
Mangrove trees grow in the salty swamps. Their roots hold the trees above the water and take in oxygen. Huge Nipa palms grow thickly among the mangroves.

Nipa palm

Sonneratia

mangrove

Bruguiera

171

The animals

green turtle

dugong

saltwater crocodile

sea snake

Deep in the rain forest, large, reddish-brown apes called orangutans move through the trees in search of fruit. These animals share their home with a variety of other creatures. Brilliantly colored hornbills fill the forest with their hooting calls. The golden flying snake is a fast-moving tree snake. It glides from tree to tree by flattening out its body.

Much of Southeast Asia is covered by tropical rain forests. Many unusual birds and animals live here, but they are not always easy to see among the thickly growing trees. Large rivers flow through the forests. These are home to all kinds of wildlife. Fish called mudskippers, which are able to breathe air, swim in the mangrove swamps around the mouths of rivers. Turtles come ashore on the sandy coasts.

Coast

Green turtles and saltwater crocodiles lay their eggs in the sand. Dugongs swim close to the shore to feed on underwater plants. Offshore, the white-breasted sea eagle and the smaller Brahmany kite scoop fish from the surface of the water.

civet

orangutan

golden flying snake

flying lizard

clouded leopard

hornbill

lesser mousedeer

loris

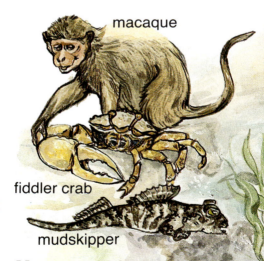

macaque

fiddler crab

mudskipper

Rain forest

Flying lizards glide through the rain forest using their outstretched "wings." The civet uses its tail to help it climb in search of fruit. The clouded leopard is also a good climber. It preys on animals such as the lesser mousedeer, which is no bigger than a hare.

Mangrove swamp

Mudskippers are fish that can live out of water for short periods of time. At low tide, they hop across the mud. Archer fish cannot live out of water. They shoot down insects with jets of water from their mouths. Macaques feed on crabs at the water's edge.

Brahmany
kite

sea eagle

tailorbird

peacock

python

Forest river

Banteng come to the forest river to drink. They are large, wild oxen with white "socks." Families of monkeys called langurs keep a lookout for huge pythons. On the bank, green peacocks display their colorful feathers. The tiny red-tailed tailorbird sews leaves together to make a nest.

silvered langur

banteng

monitor lizard

archer fish

Island

Several islands are home to animals that are found nowhere else. The babirusa, a hairless, piglike animal with four tusks, lives in Sulawesi, Indonesia. The Komodo dragon is the largest lizard in the world. The rare monkey-eating eagle lives only in the Philippines.

cockatoo

monkey-eating eagle

parrot

babirusa

red lory

Komodo dragon

anoa

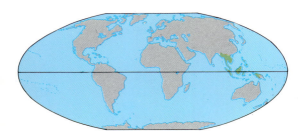

Growing and making

On the muddy Malaysian hillside, the workers slip and slide, trying to keep a foothold. Above them, in the open mine, lie piles of mud and tin ore. Using heavy hoses, the men aim powerful jets of water at the muddy ore. The ore is washed down the hill to a pool of light-brown mud below. The mud and stones are sucked up a pipe and carried along a channel where the tin ore is removed. The tin ore will now be sent off to be crushed and melted to make tin bars called ingots. Some of the ingots are used to make tin cans.

Malaysia produces a lot of tin. Oil, bauxite, iron ore, and copper are also mined in Southeast Asia. Other important products are rice, rubber, copra, cassava, and teak.

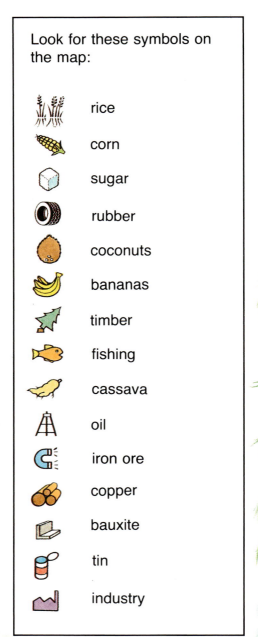

Look for these symbols on the map:

	rice
	corn
	sugar
	rubber
	coconuts
	bananas
	timber
	fishing
	cassava
	oil
	iron ore
	copper
	bauxite
	tin
	industry

Tin-mining in Malaysia
Malaysia has huge reserves of easily mined tin deposits left by flowing water. Tin is used to make a variety of products.

Teak Trees in Myanmar
Much of the world's teak comes from Myanmar, where two-thirds of the land is covered by trees. The large trees are cut down and often have to be moved by elephants. The elephants drag the heavy tree trunks to rivers, where they are floated downstream to sawmills.

Rubber growing in Indonesia

In Indonesia, rubber trees are grown on plantations. Small grooves are made in the bark of the trees every two or three days. A white gum called latex oozes out into the pail. The latex is mixed with acid to make rubber.

Rice growing in the Philippines

Rice is the main food for people in Southeast Asia. Rice needs a hot climate and lots of water to grow well. Where rainfall is light, the land is irrigated to give the rice plants enough water. These flooded fields are called paddies. On hilly ground, huge steps are cut out of the hillsides to form terraced rice paddies.

Producing copra in the Philippines

Copra is made from coconuts. The coconuts are split open and dried in the sun. Then the white flesh of the coconut is taken out of the shell and mashed to get out its rich oil. This oil is used in making soap, shampoo, and margarine, as well as a kind of rubber and brake fluid for automobiles.

175

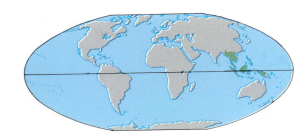

People and how they live

Puppet plays are very popular in Southeast Asia, especially in Indonesia and Malaysia. Adults and children enjoy the plays. The puppets, worked by puppeteers, may act out a story that lasts for many hours. Through these plays, the puppeteers tell the history and traditions of the countries.

There are many other popular pastimes and games. In one game, the players try to keep a wicker ball in the air by using their heads, legs, and feet. The game is called takraw in Thailand and chinlon in Myanmar. Another popular pastime is Thai-style boxing. The opponents use their feet as well as their hands. And in Malaysia and Thailand, people have kite-fighting contests with their brightly colored kites!

Most of the people of Southeast Asia live and work in rural areas. Machinery is rare in some parts, and the main crop, rice, is usually planted and harvested by hand.

Near the outskirts of Bangkok, Thailand, there is a very special shopping center—a floating market. The traders bring their boats to the market along canals called klongs.

All these people live in Southeast Asia.

Many puppets are made of leather and wood. An oil lamp throws shadows of the puppets against the screen. Behind the screen, a puppeteer moves the puppets and speaks the part of each puppet.

In Myanmar elementary schools, students sit together at long wooden desks in the classroom. To protect their skin from the sun as they go to and from school, many children wear heavy sunscreen.

In rural areas, Philippine houses are built in the traditional style. They have steep-sided roofs to keep off the heavy monsoon rains.

Bali is one of the islands of Indonesia. The island has dozens of festival days every year. Many of the festival dances are based on Bali Hinduism, the religion of the Balinese. Each hand movement in a dance has a special meaning.

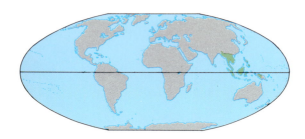

The cities

Two hundred years ago, sailing ships carried goods from Southeast Asia to places halfway around the world. The modern cities of the region have grown from the old trading centers of that time. Today they are bustling places where products from the farms, forests, and mines are exported in exchange for imports from other lands.

Cities such as Singapore and Bangkok are famous worldwide for their shops. Thousands of small manufacturers make and sell household items as well as clothing based on popular designs. The factories and shops are often run by Chinese or Indian families. The shopping areas are cluttered with colorful signs advertising the products.

Jakarta is the capital city of Indonesia. It is one of the most crowded cities in Southeast Asia. In the center of the city is the old town, built by the Dutch about 300 years ago. Around this area, modern office buildings and many new roads have been built. ⇩⇩

The capital city of Thailand is Krung Thep, which means "City of Angels." Foreigners call the city **Bangkok.** The old part of the city has many magnificent palaces and hundreds of beautiful Buddhist temples. But the city's main business center is several miles to the east. ⇨

Many puppets are made of leather and wood. An oil lamp throws shadows of the puppets against the screen. Behind the screen, a puppeteer moves the puppets and speaks the part of each puppet.

In Myanmar elementary schools, students sit together at long wooden desks in the classroom. To protect their skin from the sun as they go to and from school, many children wear heavy sunscreen.

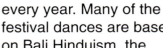

In rural areas, Philippine houses are built in the traditional style. They have steep-sided roofs to keep off the heavy monsoon rains.

Bali is one of the islands of Indonesia. The island has dozens of festival days every year. Many of the festival dances are based on Bali Hinduism, the religion of the Balinese. Each hand movement in a dance has a special meaning.

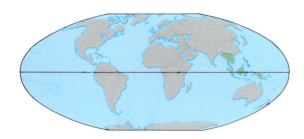

The cities

Two hundred years ago, sailing ships carried goods from Southeast Asia to places halfway around the world. The modern cities of the region have grown from the old trading centers of that time. Today they are bustling places where products from the farms, forests, and mines are exported in exchange for imports from other lands.

Cities such as Singapore and Bangkok are famous worldwide for their shops. Thousands of small manufacturers make and sell household items as well as clothing based on popular designs. The factories and shops are often run by Chinese or Indian families. The shopping areas are cluttered with colorful signs advertising the products.

Jakarta is the capital city of Indonesia. It is one of the most crowded cities in Southeast Asia. In the center of the city is the old town, built by the Dutch about 300 years ago. Around this area, modern office buildings and many new roads have been built. ⬇︎

The capital city of Thailand is Krung Thep, which means "City of Angels." Foreigners call the city **Bangkok.** The old part of the city has many magnificent palaces and hundreds of beautiful Buddhist temples. But the city's main business center is several miles to the east. ➪

⇑
The capital of Vietnam is **Hanoi.** This city is in the delta of the Red River in the northern part of the country. Parts of Hanoi were damaged by bombs during the Vietnam War, from 1957 to 1975. Some of the city has been carefully rebuilt. These girls are riding down Hanoi Street.

⇑
Yangon is the capital city and main port of Myanmar. Its most famous building is the Shwe Dagon pagoda. The building's domes are covered with gold. The markets in Yangon sell many locally made items, jewelry, and carvings made from the beautiful stone called jade.

Singapore is one of the world's busiest ports. Singapore is also an important business city, where many international companies have their offices. ⇒

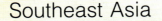

In the Ring of Fire

The sky is cloudless and the sea is calm as the ship makes its way slowly out of the harbor on Sulawesi. This is the start of its journey through part of the Ring of Fire. The Ring of Fire is the name given to a chain of hundreds of active volcanoes that almost encircle the Pacific Ocean.

At a safe distance from the shore, the crew hoists the sails and the ship speeds on. The ship is a black-sailed ship called a prahu. This is the traditional sailing ship of the Bugis islanders who are sea traders. For thousands of years, the Bugis traded widely among the thousands of small islands of Indonesia, but they trade mainly between the larger islands of Sulawesi, Java, and Borneo.

As the prahu leaves the protection of the shore, and sails out into the Banda Sea, dolphins leap near the ship. It is heading for the volcanic island of Banda.

Each shipbuilder uses the special shape of the timber in the design of a ship. So, although every prahu has two tall masts and a low, curved, timber hull, no two prahus are ever exactly alike.

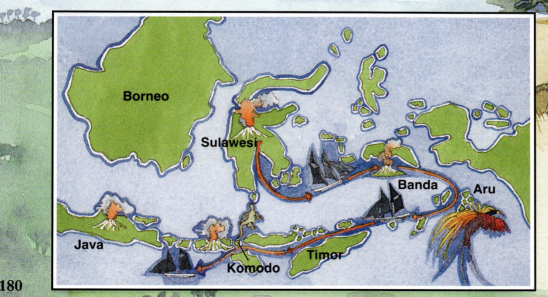

On Komodo Island, huge lizards called Komodo dragons sniff out their prey. Komodo dragons have long claws, sharp teeth, and are very strong. They will eat animals such as goats and small deer.

At Banda the ship is loaded with red nutmegs. These will be ground into a rich fruity spice.

After Banda, the prahu sets sail for the island of Aru. As the ship approaches the island, excited voices are heard on one of the fishing boats anchored on the coral reef. A diver has just found a magnificent pearl in an oyster. Such natural pearls are rare. But the shell of the golden-lipped oyster is also valuable for its beautiful mother-of-pearl.

With its hold full of nutmeg and shells, the prahu heads for Java. From Java, it will sail to other islands, unloading cargo and taking on new cargo as it goes. It may travel thousands of miles (kilometers), past many islands topped by towering volcanoes, but it will still have sailed only a tiny part of the way around the great Pacific Ring of Fire.

In the forests of Aru lives the greater bird of paradise. The male bird makes a display of its long tail feathers.

Smoke billows constantly from the cone of Banda's single active volcano, but eruptions take place only about once every hundred years.

Welcome to Africa

Africa is a huge continent mostly surrounded by water. The Atlantic and the Indian oceans wash much of its coastline but Africa also touches the Mediterranean and the Red seas.

Africa is the second largest continent in the world, after Asia. It stretches southward from the Mediterranean across the equator and into the southern half of the world. Africa has a variety of natural features—beautiful coasts, tropical rain forests, and spectacular waterfalls. The huge Sahara is the world's largest desert, and the Nile is the world's longest river. Some of the continent is grassland where giraffes, lions, and zebras live.

There are more than fifty countries in Africa, more than on any other continent. More than 800 languages are spoken by the different groups of peoples who live there.

Many modern cities are centers of trade and government.

Huge areas of grassland are set aside as national parks.

Equator

Traditional dances are often performed to the music of many drums.

In the northern desert regions, both trucks and camels transport goods.

Both traditional and modern lifestyles are found in African villages.

Women often harvest the crops and grind the grain by hand.

The old market of Marrakech in Morocco is a famous trading place.

183

The countries

Africa covers about one-fifth of the world's land area. It is the second largest continent, after Asia. There are fifty-three independent countries in Africa. The Arab countries in the north are separated from the rest of Africa by the Sahara.

Africa has a large population. Some areas with rich soil are overcrowded. Other parts, such as the Sahara, have very few people.

The history

In ancient times, North Africa was closely linked with Europe across the Mediterranean Sea. But Europeans knew little about the large African kingdoms south of the burning-hot Sahara.

From the 1400's, European explorers sailed down the coasts of Africa. They were followed in the 1500's by traders who took slaves from Africa to the Americas. The slave trade was stopped in the 1800's. In the late 1800's, Europeans divided Africa into more than fifty countries. They ruled these countries as colonies. After World War II, the African people demanded their independence.

The government

After independence, one-party political systems were established in many African countries. But by the early 1990's, a number of these countries adopted multiparty systems.

Algeria Angola Benin

Botswana Burkina Faso Burundi

Cameroon Cape Verde Central African Republic

Chad Comoros Cote d'Ivoire Democratic Republic of Congo Djibouti Egypt

Equatorial Guinea Eritrea Ethiopia Gabon Gambia Ghana

Guinea Guinea-Bissau Kenya Lesotho Liberia

Libya Madagascar Malawi Mali Mauritania Mauritius

Morocco Mozambique Namibia Niger Nigeria Republic of the Congo

Rwanda São Tomé and Príncipe Senegal Seychelles Sierra Leone

Somalia South Africa Sudan Swaziland Tanzania

Togo Tunisia Uganda Zambia Zimbabwe

184

Facts about Africa
There are fifty-three independent countries in the region.
Area: 11,678,000 square miles (30,246,000 sq. km).
Population: About 875,122,000.
Largest country: Sudan.
Highest mountain: Kilimanjaro, in Tanzania, is 19,340 feet (5,895 m) high.
Longest river: The Nile, which flows from the highlands of East Africa north through Sudan and Egypt, is 4,145 miles (6,671 km) long.

Atlantic Ocean

Algiers

Casablanca ● ■ Rabat
MOROCCO

TUNISIA
Tripoli ■

ALGERIA

Alexandria ●
■ Cairo

LIBYA

EGYPT

Western Sahara

MAURITANIA

MALI

NIGER

CHAD

SUDAN

Khartoum ■

ERITREA

CAPE VERDE

SENEGAL

GAMBIA

GUINEA-BISSAU

GUINEA

BURKINA FASO

● Kano

NIGERIA

DJIBOUTI

● Addis Ababa

ETHIOPIA

SIERRA LEONE

COTE D'IVOIRE

BENIN

GHANA

LIBERIA

TOGO

Abuja ■

Lagos

CAMEROON

CENTRAL AFRICAN REPUBLIC

SOMALIA

SÃO TOMÉ and PRÍNCIPE

EQUATORIAL GUINEA

GABON

DEMOCRATIC REPUBLIC OF CONGO

UGANDA

RWANDA

KENYA

Nairobi ■

Indian Ocean

Brazzaville ■

REPUBLIC OF THE CONGO

Kinshasa ■

BURUNDI

TANZANIA

SEYCHELLES

■ Luanda

ANGOLA

ZAMBIA

MALAWI

MOZAMBIQUE

COMOROS

ZIMBABWE

MADAGASCAR

NAMIBIA

BOTSWANA

MAURITIUS

Pretoria ■
Johannesburg ●

SWAZILAND

SOUTH AFRICA

LESOTHO

Cape Town ●

The wealth

Many countries in Africa are very poor, and most of the people struggle to grow enough crops to feed their families.

Some countries in Africa are rich in minerals. The government controls the mining industry in several African nations.

The governments of most African countries are trying to build more factories and bring farming methods up to date in order to create more wealth.

185

Looking at the land

Africa is a huge continent with all kinds of scenery. In the north lies the Sahara, the largest desert in the world. But Africa also has plenty of water. Four of its rivers are the Nile, the Congo, the Niger, and the Zambezi. Victoria Falls is on the Zambezi River. It is a massive waterfall.

Near the rivers, the land is fertile and many plants and trees grow. One of the largest artificial lakes in the world, Lake Nasser, has formed behind the Aswan High Dam on the Nile River. Most of Africa's large lakes are in the eastern regions. Here, chains of long, deep lakes have formed in the valleys.

There are also grasslands called savannas in eastern Africa, where herds of wild animals roam. Mount Kilimanjaro can be seen in the distance. It is Africa's highest peak and is an extinct volcano.

The **Sahara** is the world's largest desert. It covers an area almost the size of the United States. In some places in the Sahara, there are sand dunes that are hundreds of feet high. But only part of the desert is covered by sand. Most is bare, rocky uplands and gravel plains.

Victoria Falls is on the Zambezi River. Like Lake Victoria, it was named after the British Queen Victoria. The water crashes 355 feet (108 m) over a cliff, with a thundering roar. The African name for the Falls is Mosi oa Tunya, which means "the Smoke that Thunders."

The **Nile** is the longest river in the world. Its waters are used to irrigate millions of acres of land.

Mount Kilimanjaro, in Tanzania, is Africa's highest mountain. It is a dead, or extinct, volcano that rises 19,331 feet (5,892 m) above sea level. It is so high that it is always capped with ice and snow, even though it is close to the equator. Some large glaciers cover the slopes of the peak.

In southern Africa there is a large high plain, or plateau. The edge of the plateau tilts up like the rim of a saucer. In places, rivers have worn deep valleys like jagged teeth into this rim. This jagged rim is called the **Drakensberg,** which means "Dragon Mountain."

Nile

Lake Nasser

Sahara

Niger

Congo

Kilimanjaro

Lake Victoria

Victoria Falls

Zambezi

Drakensberg

The plants

date
palm

tamarisk

The northern half of Africa is mainly a huge desert region. Here, before a rain, dark gray clouds roll across the sky, making shadows on the dry land. Then the rain comes. Great drops of water beat down upon the dusty soil. It rains heavily for just a short time, but the rain transforms the land. Where there was once only hard ground, brightly colored flowering plants spring up. New grasses grow and shrubs sprout. The plants had waited as seeds in the ground for the rain to come. When the new plants grow, they will produce more seeds. These may have to wait for months, or even years, for the next rainfall.

In an area along the Congo River, the weather is very different. In some parts, there is rain almost every day, and a huge, green rain forest has grown. But over most of Africa there is just enough rain to allow grasses and some tough trees to grow. The grassland is called a savanna.

Acacia

Convolvulus

Desert

In Africa's great Sahara, plants such as the acacia and the tamarisk survive in very dry conditions. Near oases, where water is found, there are date palms and blue convolvuluses.

afara
tree

orchid

liana

ebony
tree

palm

baobab
tree

fern

Rain forest

Forests stretch across Africa, from Mozambique to Sierra Leone, with an exciting variety of trees. Many of the tallest trees have strong roots sticking out from their trunks to help support them. Climbing palms and creepers and many ferns and orchids grow on the trees.

Grassland

Between forest and desert are huge areas of grasslands, or savannas. Here the hot sun often burns the grasses and creates fires. Some trees can survive fire. Coral tree seeds need to be scorched before they will grow.

188

Marshland

The banks of Africa's lakes and long rivers are often swampy. Some are lined with feathery reeds or the papyrus plant with its tufted heads. Open water may become covered with floating plants, such as water lettuce and water hyacinth.

reed

papyrus

water hyacinth

water lettuce

Mountain

Many different types of plants grow in Africa's high regions. Above the forests are bamboo thickets. Higher up is a strange landscape of short grasses, everlasting flowers, giant groundsels, and lobelias. Mosses and lichens grow on the highest mountains.

giant groundsel

giant Lobelia

everlasting flower

candelabrum tree

coral tree

fireball lily

Pennisetum

189

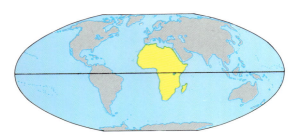

Africa

The animals

crowned eagle

colobus monkey

leopard

gorilla

Each year, many people visit the rough grassland of the Amboseli National Park in Kenya. They travel in heavy jeeps, following rough tracks or sometimes driving a path through knee-high grass, to catch sight of the wild animals that live here. Sometimes they see a pride of lions. The male lion lazes in the shade while his mate and the other lionesses prowl back and forth. In the distance there are often herds of grazing animals—wildebeest, gazelles, and zebra.

Visitors to the national parks learn a lot by watching these wild animals in their natural habitat. People are not allowed to hunt the animals that live in the national parks.

Africa's grasslands, forests, and lakes are all rich in wildlife. Even in the great dry deserts there are all kinds of interesting creatures.

mandrill

red striped squirrel

Grassland

Africa's plains provide food for many grasseaters, such as the graceful impala, the zebra, and the topi. The giraffe and the rhinoceros eat the leaves of trees. The hunters of the plains include the hyena and the cheetah.

elephant

giraffe

impala

gazelle

wildebeest

topi

zebra

hyena

rhinoceros

cheetah

lion

Forest
Gorillas are the largest apes. They travel in groups through the rain forest, looking for buds, leaves, and fruit to eat. Mandrills travel in groups, too. The male mandrill has blue cheeks and a flat, red nose. The leopard and the crowned eagle are both hunters. They prey on small forest animals, such as the red striped squirrel and the colobus monkey.

190

Northern desert

In the Sahara, the large-eared fennec fox hides by day and hunts by night. So do some snakes, such as the saw-scaled viper, which moves sideways across the sand. Scorpions and skinks live in the sand.

scorpion

fennec fox

saw-scaled viper

skink

hippopotamus

flamingo

lily trotter

Lake

Many of Africa's lakes are home to crocodiles. Flamingos wade in the shallows. The spreading feet of the lily trotter help it walk across floating plants.

crocodile

ring-tailed lemur

ruffed lemur

chameleon

Madagascar

On the island of Madagascar live many animals that are found nowhere else on earth. Among them are the lemurs, which are furry, monkeylike creatures. The largest chameleons in the world also live here.

191

Growing and making

The sun beats down. Clouds of dust rise up from the dry soil as the woman hoes between the young plants. The baby tied to her back is rocked to sleep as the mother works. Most people living in Africa work on the land. Some herd animals while others grow crops. Women often work in the fields, and much of the work is done with simple tools. This means that farmers work slowly and cannot plant or harvest large crops. Children are expected to help before they go to school. They will be up early feeding chickens, milking the goat, or fetching water from the well for the young corn plants.

In most African countries there are also large farms and plantations where modern machinery is used. Bananas, coffee, cotton, tea, and cocoa beans are grown here. Many of these products are sold to countries all over the world.

Look for these symbols on the map:

- cattle
- sheep
- cotton
- tea
- coffee
- peanuts
- cocoa
- bananas
- cassava
- oil
- natural gas
- gold
- diamonds
- copper
- industry

Coffee

At harvest time, many people work on the coffee plantations. All the ripe berries on the coffee tree must be picked by hand. Then they are sorted and processed.

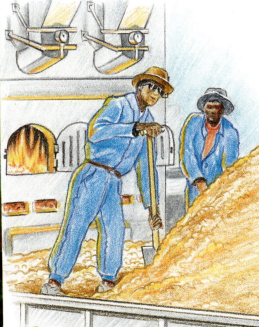

Peanuts

Peanuts are grown in the light, sandy soil of Nigeria. Peanuts contain oil and protein, and are good food for people. Peanut shells are ground into powder to make fertilizer and plastics.

Oil and gas

In the north of Africa lie the Arab countries, including Algeria and Libya. These lands are rich in oil and natural gas. Wells have been drilled in the desert to extract these riches.

Farming

In many African countries, there is very little farm machinery. Most farmers work with simple, hand-held tools and use oxen instead of tractors. In many areas, the soil is poor and the farmers struggle to grow enough to eat.

Mining

Miners dig for gold and diamonds in South Africa. The biggest diamond ever found came from a mine near Pretoria. It was as big as a person's fist.

193

Africa

People and how they live

Many African people live in small villages in rural areas. Most villages have a central square where people can gather to meet and talk. Here the scene is often colorful. Most villagers like to wear traditional African clothing, with bold, bright colors. And patterned necklaces, bracelets, and earrings are everyday wear for some Africans.

Life for many African people is hard. Both men and women work long hours at farming to make a living. And lots of children leave school after only a few years to help their families. The cities provide more schools and better medical care than the rural areas. But many cities also have a great number of unemployed people.

Although many African countries are becoming more modern, many people still have a traditional way of life. They remain loyal to the family and to their village, even if they go away to the city to work or to a college or university. And they enjoy traditional songs and dances that retell the hunting stories of long ago.

In many West African villages, women are in charge of the home and the farm. They work on the land to grow food. In some places, scientists are now working to help the women. They suggest the best seeds and crops to grow in poor, dry soil.

People of many nationalities live and work in Africa's modern cities.

Pygmies are a group of small people living in central Africa. They have a simple lifestyle, hunting or gathering the food in the rain forests.

194

The Bedouins are a group of Arab people. Those who follow their traditional way of life are nomads. They travel across the deserts of northern Africa looking for fresh water or grassland for their camels, goats, and sheep. They live in tents and trade meat and dairy products in villages for goods.

All these people live in Africa.

Most Kenyans have adapted to life in a modern country, but many traditions remain. This group of Maasai is performing a traditional dance, which has not changed in hundreds of years.

195

The cities

Many cities and towns in Africa are huge distances apart. Some are linked by railroads, but others are reached at the end of a long, dusty drive on dirt roads or, in some cases, by riverboat. Few people in Africa can afford to travel by air. Kinshasa, the capital city of the Democratic Republic of Congo, has an important location on the Congo River. This mighty river and its tributaries flow through thick forests, reaching out to hundreds of inland towns. Goods are brought to Kinshasa by truck from the seaports on the coast. There they are piled onto small riverboats and barges to make the journey upstream. Kinshasa has become a busy center of trade for goods moving in all directions.

Kano is the major city in northern Nigeria. At one time it was an important caravan center. Outside the walls of the old city, a new city has been built. It has factories and an international airport.

Cairo is the capital of Egypt. It is the largest city in Africa and also one of the oldest. Old Cairo is a maze of crooked streets, markets called bazaars, old stone houses, and hundreds of mosques where Muslims pray. To the north is new Cairo, the modern part of the city.

↑

Nairobi, the capital of Kenya, is the most important commercial center in eastern Africa. The central area of the city has many modern buildings, and its main streets are lined with trees. The Kenyan government is a major employer in Nairobi. Industry and tourism are also important parts of the city's economy.

Johannesburg is the most important manufacturing city in South Africa. It lies in the center of a rich gold field. The city began in 1886, when gold was first discovered in the area. Today, both gold and diamonds are mined nearby, as are coal, iron, and other minerals. These resources have led to the growth of many industries. ↓↓

↑

The seaport of **Dakar** is the capital of Senegal. Its harbor is one of the busiest in Africa. Ships leave here for many other African countries and for France. They carry peanuts, minerals, and products made from fish. Dakar's colorful markets are famous for spices and flowers.

↑ **Zanzibar** is the main city on Zanzibar Island, which is part of Tanzania. In the 1800's, Zanzibar was famous for its slave markets. Now the port is a center of trade along the East African coast. The city exports cloves, chili peppers, coconut oil, and fruit.

Down the Great Rift Valley

The safari sets off from Nairobi in the morning. Everyone is eager to make the journey to the Masai Mara game reserve and to see the wildlife that lives there.

The game reserve lies to the west of the Great Rift Valley. This valley was formed millions of years ago when movements deep inside the earth split the earth's crust. It is a huge depression in the earth. The road to the valley floor winds steeply downhill. The valley is not flat, but is dotted with hills. These are volcanoes, and thirty of them are still active.

Well-worn tracks lead to fresh water springs at a lake's edge. These are the tracks of lions, rhinoceros, zebra, and antelope that come to drink at dusk.

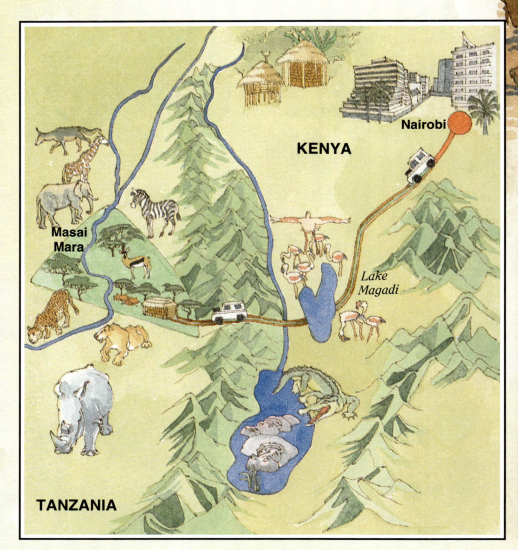

The Ngong Hills are a line of volcanic peaks. It has been thousands of years since they last erupted, and their craters are now worn into rounded, green humps.

198

An hour after passing the Ngong Hills, the safari reaches Lake Magadi, the Soda Lake. No plants can survive the heat of this volcanic lake with its hot springs. But the flamingos enjoy the fish that manage to live here. Once a year, up to three million of these elegant pink birds arrive to breed.

It is dark before the jeep bumps its way down the rough track that leads to the lodge of Maasi Mara. Here, the group will spend the night, eating by the campfire and sleeping in tents under the stars.

The sky is still dark as the jeep leaves the lodge the next day. Soon the safari is well into the game reserve, driving slowly. Everyone is on the lookout, for at this early hour, the cheetah, the hyena, and the lioness awake and stalk their prey.

The day is filled with excitement. The reserve is dotted with herds of grazing wildebeest, gazelles, zebra, and impala. The party surprises a pride of lions ripping the last flesh from the morning's kill. Nearby, a cheetah plays with its cubs. In the shade of a clump of thorn bushes, an elephant strips bark for its young, while giraffes chew the thorny branches above.

The game reserve has wandering herds of wild animals.

The safari passes a young Maasi moving his cattle from one grazing ground to another. He carries a long spear to defend himself and his herd from wild animals.

That night the people sit and talk over the day's adventures. Everyone knows that the life of the game reserve is threatened. Poachers trap the animals, and the land is poor from overuse. The travelers hope that this wild country will not be destroyed by its greatest enemy—people.

199

Welcome to Australia, New Zealand, and the Pacific Islands

The Pacific Ocean is the world's largest ocean. It contains more than 30,000 islands, including the islands of New Zealand. Australia is bordered by the Indian and Pacific oceans.

Australia is so large that it spans an area from just south of the equator to the northernmost waters of the Antarctic Ocean. The climate varies from tropical monsoon weather in the north, to cold winters in the south.

Australia has hot, dry land in the interior with many deserts, but coastal mountains and plains provide rich grassland and wooded areas. Some Australian animals, such as the kangaroo and the koala, are quite different from any other creatures in the world.

New Zealand lies about 1,000 miles (1,600 km) southeast of Australia. Some of its famous sights are the springs and geysers, where hot, steamy water shoots out of the ground at great speed.

Surfing is one of the most popular sports in Australia and New Zealand.

Equator

Sheep are New Zealand's most important farm animals.

Sydney Opera House overlooks
Sydney's beautiful harbor.

The Great Barrier Reef is
the world's largest coral reef.

Ayers Rock, in central Australia, has been
worn into a rounded shape by the wind.

Farmers raise cattle in many
parts of Australia.

Kangaroos live in most
parts of Australia.

The countries

This region is made up of Australia, New Zealand, and the Pacific Islands. Australia's nearest neighbors are the countries of Southeast Asia.

New Zealand is made up of two big islands and several small ones. Tasmania is also an island, but it is one of the states of Australia, too.

Australia

Fiji

Kiribati

Marshall Islands

Micronesia

Nauru

New Zealand

Palau

PAPUA NEW GUINEA

Port Moresby

Pacific Ocean

Darwin

AUSTRALIA

Alice Springs

Lake Eyre

Brisbane

Darling

Indian Ocean

Perth

Adelaide

Murray

Sydney

Canberra

Melbourne

Tasman Sea

Hobart

Papua New Guinea

Samoa

The history

The first people to live in Australia were the Aborigines. They have been living there for at least 40,000 years. The European explorer Captain Cook visited Australia in 1770. He claimed the land as a British colony. In later years, convicts were sent there to serve their prison sentences. As groups of Europeans settled in Australia, most of the Aborigines were killed in fighting or by diseases brought by the settlers. Later, farmers and gold prospectors explored and settled the land.

These settlers also spread to New Zealand. Since those times immigrants from all over Europe and Asia have come to Australia and New Zealand and have formed a strong workforce.

202

The wealth

Australia is rich in natural resources. It has been able to make the most of these resources because its farming and mining industries are very up to date and efficient. New Zealand has always depended on its farming as the main source of its wealth.

Even though Australia and New Zealand are far away from Europe and the United States, they still sell many farm products to these places. Australia also exports minerals to all parts of the world.

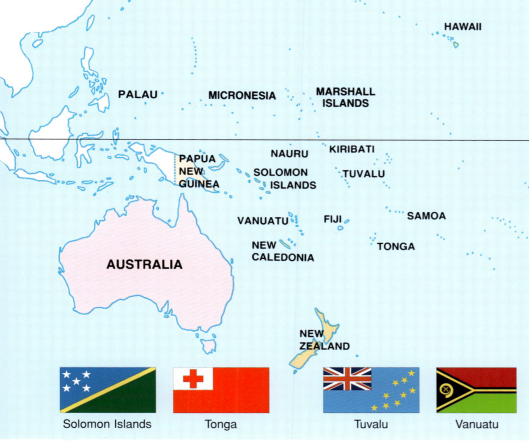

The Pacific Islands are made up of three main groups. These are Polynesia, Melanesia, and Micronesia. Within these groups there are many small islands. Australia is the largest country in this area.

The group of islands called Hawaii is a state of the United States. Like many of the other Pacific Islands, Hawaii earns money from tourism. Mining takes place on several islands, including Nauru, Fiji, and New Caledonia. But on some islands, many people earn little or no money.

Solomon Islands   Tonga   Tuvalu   Vanuatu

The government

In 1901, Australia stopped being a British colony and became an independent country. New Zealand became independent in 1907. But both still belong to the group of countries in the British Commonwealth.

Australia and New Zealand are monarchies. The head of state is Queen Elizabeth II of Britain. She is represented in both countries by a Governor-General, who acts as head of state. The countries are governed by their prime ministers and parliaments, who are elected by the people.

Many other Pacific Islands that were once governed by Britain, France, New Zealand, or the United States now largely govern themselves.

Auckland

NEW ZEALAND   Wellington

Facts about Australia, New Zealand, and the Pacific Islands

There are fourteen independent countries in the region.

Area: 3,288,207 square miles (8,518,670 sq. km).

Population: About 31,236,000.

Largest country: Australia.

Highest mountain: Mount Wilhelm, in Papua New Guinea, is 14,793 feet (4,509 m) high.

Longest river: The Darling River in Australia, which flows into the Murray River, is 1,702 miles (2,739 km) long. But most of the Darling is dry in winter. The Murray flows all year. It is 1,609 miles (2,589 km) long.

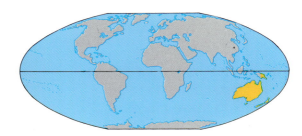

Looking at the land

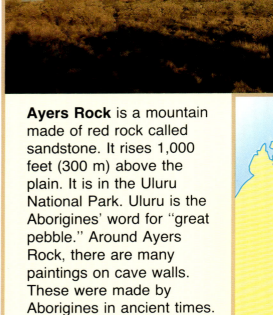

Ayers Rock is a mountain made of red rock called sandstone. It rises 1,000 feet (300 m) above the plain. It is in the Uluru National Park. Uluru is the Aborigines' word for "great pebble." Around Ayers Rock, there are many paintings on cave walls. These were made by Aborigines in ancient times.

Pacific Ocean

Great Barrier Reef

Ayers Rock

Great Victoria Desert

Great Dividing Range

The **Great Victoria Desert** is one of many deserts that cover about a third of Australia. Near its center are several small lakes that are usually dry. Few people live in these sunbaked areas. The desert is made up of sand dunes that are constantly shifting in the wind.

The **Great Barrier Reef** is the world's largest coral reef. It stretches about 1,240 miles (2,000 km) along the northeastern coast of Australia.

The North Island of New Zealand has many volcanoes. There are also hot springs and geysers, such as **Pohutu Geyser,** at Rotorua. Three or four times a day the geyser shoots a jet of hot water and steam into the air.

Pohutu Geyser

Much of Australia is low and flat. The highest land lies near the east coast. This is called the Great Dividing Range. Most rain falls along the east coast and this land is fertile for growing crops and fruit. West of the Great Dividing Range, central Australia is flat and dry. Some rivers dry up for long periods each summer. Sheep and cattle graze here, but crops, apart from grass, will not grow. Farther west, over one-third of Australia is a windswept desert of sand and small stones.

Much of New Zealand is green and fertile. Crops and fruit are grown in many parts of the country and sheep and dairy cattle graze on the rich pasture land. There are thick forests and many rivers and lakes. On North Island there are volcanoes and hot springs.

In the warm seas around Australia, coral islands have formed slowly over thousands of years. The Great Barrier Reef off the northeast coast of Australia is the world's largest coral reef. Brightly colored plants and fish live in the turquoise waters around the reef.

Kilauea is a large, active volcano on Hawaii. Although its huge crater is almost two miles (3 km) wide, Kilauea is only part of a larger volcano, Mauna Loa. Whenever Kilauea erupts, the people nearby must move to safety.

Hawaii is one of a group of 132 islands that make up the state of Hawaii. All the islands were formed by volcanoes.

Many **coral islands** are atolls. These are coral reefs that are shaped like rings or horseshoes. Inside the horseshoe is a lagoon. One or more channels connect the lagoon to the open sea.

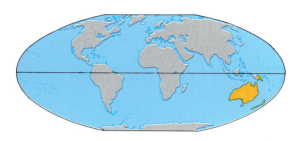

The plants

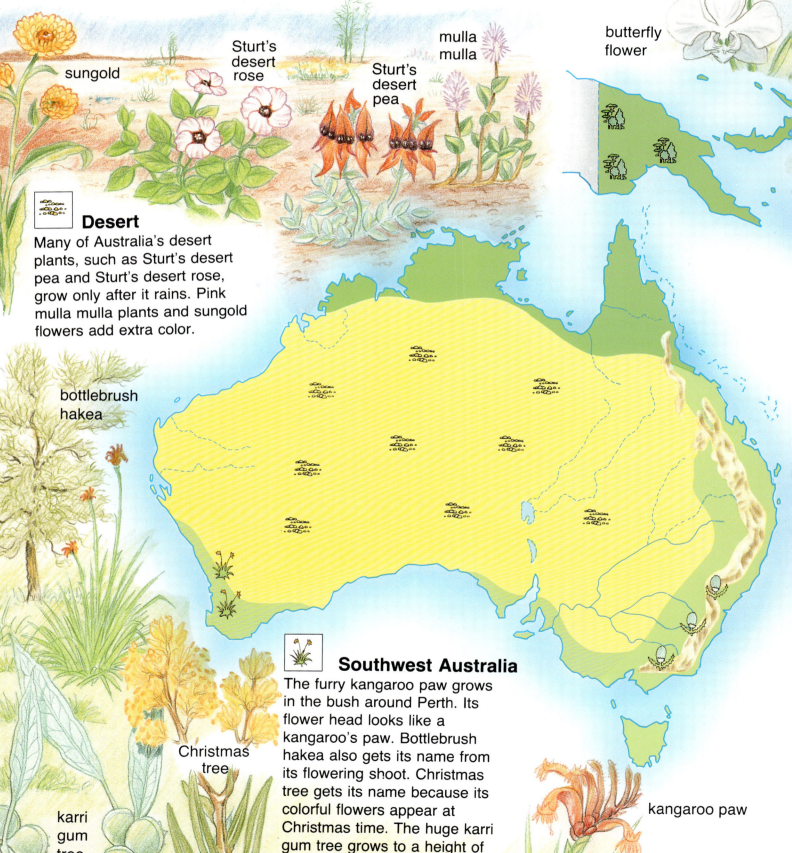

sungold

Sturt's desert rose

Sturt's desert pea

mulla mulla

butterfly flower

Desert
Many of Australia's desert plants, such as Sturt's desert pea and Sturt's desert rose, grow only after it rains. Pink mulla mulla plants and sungold flowers add extra color.

bottlebrush hakea

Christmas tree

karri gum tree

Southwest Australia
The furry kangaroo paw grows in the bush around Perth. Its flower head looks like a kangaroo's paw. Bottlebrush hakea also gets its name from its flowering shoot. Christmas tree gets its name because its colorful flowers appear at Christmas time. The huge karri gum tree grows to a height of nearly 250 feet (75 m).

kangaroo paw

screw
pine

cycad

fringe lily

Papua New Guinea

The strange cycad grows in the mountain forests of Papua New Guinea. Scientists think it can live for thousands of years. Screw pines have roots that act like props to support the trunk. The butterfly flower attracts real butterflies because its petals nod like flying butterflies. The flowers of the fringe lily have hairy-edged petals.

Imagine a place where many years may pass without a single drop of rain! Only the toughest plants can survive in the scorching center of Australia. Two flowering plants that do survive are named after another tough survivor, the explorer Charles Sturt. The seeds of the Sturt's desert pea lie in the ground for years waiting for rain. Then they quickly grow and bloom with waxy red flowers. The Sturt's desert rose survives in the same way. It has pink petals with dark red centers. Refreshed by the rain, a carpet of sungold flowers will spring up. This plant, which has scented leaves, is also known as the golden paper daisy.

Closer to the coast, there are thousands of different flowers and many types of trees. The gum tree, or eucalyptus, is probably the best-known Australian tree.

golden wattle

waratah

Christmas bell

silver banksia

Southeast Australia

The golden wattle is Australia's national flower. It grows into a small tree. The waratah has big, deep-red flowers. The Aborigines gave the plant its name, which means "seen from afar" in their language. Also growing around Sydney are the smaller red flowers called Christmas bells. They flower in December. The silver banksia, or tree honeysuckle, is a shrub with spiky flowers.

cabbage tree

New Zealand

The kowhai, New Zealand's national flower, was given its name by the Maoris. Cabbage trees were named by European settlers who found they could eat the young shoots. These palmlike trees often grow among clumps of toe-toe grass. Tree daisies are shrubs with daisylike flowers.

tree daisy

toe-toe grass

kowhai

207

The animals

galah

parakeet

dingo

emu

red kangaroo

rabbit-eared bandicoot

spotted cuscus

sugar glider

Outback

In Australia's outback, the wild dog, or dingo, hunts in packs. The emu is too large and heavy to fly, but it can run very fast. The rabbit-eared bandicoot has sharp hearing and catches small animals and insects with its long snout.

kookaburra

wallaby

platypus

Tasmanian devil

tiger cat

Tasmania

Tasmania is the home of the bearlike Tasmanian devil. The platypus is also found in Tasmanian rivers. This strange creature has a ducklike bill, a furry body, and webbed feet. The laughing kookaburra is a large kingfisher that feeds on lizards, worms, and beetles.

bird of paradise

bowerbird

echidna

Papua New Guinea

In Papua New Guinea's tropical forests, there are many colorful birds of paradise. The males hold out their feathers in marvelous displays to attract mates. The bowerbird builds a special shelter of twigs and grasses. It collects many kinds of brightly colored objects to place inside.

Gum tree forest

Most forest animals sleep during the day and come out at night to feed. Many are marsupials, which means they carry their young in a pouch. The koala eats the leaves of certain gum trees. The sugar glider, a kind of flying squirrel, likes nectar, soft fruit, and insects. The spotted tiger cat is a good tree climber and hunts small animals.

koala

pygmy glider

Huge areas of dry grassland and desert in central Australia are called the outback. The kangaroo, one of Australia's best-known animals, lives here, feeding on grasses and leaves. Flocks of green and blue parakeets fly down to the water holes to drink. Lovely pink and gray galahs, a type of cockatoo, perch in the trees. Nearer the coast, it is wet and warm, and all kinds of interesting forest creatures live there. Off the Queensland coast is the Great Barrier Reef, with many beautiful underwater animals.

Australia became a separate continent about 200 million years ago. Its animals developed differently from those on other continents. Today Australia has many fascinating wild animals that are found nowhere else in the world.

mako shark

manta ray

Australian coast

Off the coast of Australia, mako sharks chase fish so fast that they often leap out of the water. Sometimes, great white sharks come close to the shore. The Pacific manta ray is a huge fish. The blue-ringed octopus is small and lives in rock pools. Its poisonous bite can kill people.

great white shark

blue-ringed octopus

sea horse

kakapo

kea

New Zealand

New Zealand has some very rare birds, such as the kakapo, the kea, and the kiwi. Kiwis can't fly. They use their long bills to search for food in the soil. The kea is a large, fierce parrot. Lizards called tuataras can live for more than 100 years.

kiwi

tuatara

209

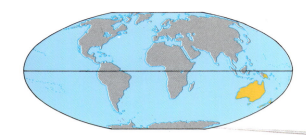

Growing and making

Banana growing in Papua New Guinea

In Papua New Guinea the tiny banana plants are set out in rows. First, tightly rolled leaves grow, followed by buds that will turn into flowers. There are ten to twenty bananas in each bunch, called a "hand." The bananas are picked and shipped while still green.

Mining in Australia

One of the world's richest supplies of bauxite is in Western Australia. Bauxite is mined, then crushed and heated to make aluminum. Aluminum does not rust and is easily bent into different shapes. It is used to make cans, window frames and airplanes.

Look for these symbols on the map:

- 🌾 wheat
- 🐂 cattle
- 🐑 sheep
- 🥛 dairy products
- 🍎 fruits
- 🍇 grapes
- 🧊 sugar
- 🥥 coconuts
- 🍌 bananas
- 🛢️ oil
- 🧲 iron ore
- 🟤 copper
- bauxite
- coal
- 🏭 industry
- ⚡ hydroelectricity
- nickel

The farmer turns over the fleece carefully, measuring its weight and inspecting it for its length and soft texture. He knows that the shearers are clipping the heavy fleece as close to the sheep's skin as they can. They remove each fleece in one piece. The shearers work very fast. A skillful shearer can shear 200 sheep or more in a day. This seems like a lot, but there are more than 200 million sheep in Australia and New Zealand to shear each year! Later, the wool will be packed into bales and sent to be graded and sold.

Australia produces more wool than any other country. And New Zealand is a major wool exporter, too. Other important agricultural products in the region include wheat, fruit, beef, and dairy products.

Nickel mining in New Caledonia

Large amounts of nickel ore are mined in New Caledonia. The ore is ground to a powder, squeezed into lumps, and then melted down and set, or cast, into bars called ingots. The ingots are exported all over the world for use in making stainless steel and coins.

Dairy farming in New Zealand

The grass in New Zealand grows all year round. It is perfect for grazing dairy cattle. About three million cows produce milk that is made into butter and cheese. Butter is made from cream that is stirred around in a churn until it becomes hard. The buttermilk is drained off, and the butter is washed and pumped out of the churn in a long ribbon, which is then cut up and wrapped.

211

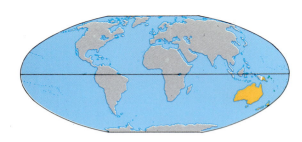

People and how they live

It has been only 200 years since European settlers first landed in Australia. From that time, people from many other countries have gone there to live. People of many nationalities have joined the original inhabitants of Australia, the Aborigines, and those of New Zealand, the Maoris.

Although Australia is a vast country, most of the people live in the towns and cities around the coasts. Areas that are a long way from the cities, usually inland, are called the outback. The outback can be desert or grassland. Families who live on sheep and cattle ranches are often many miles from their nearest neighbors. Children get their lessons at home on the computer because it is too far to travel to a school. The doctor may have to visit patients by plane. Neighbors are used to driving long distances to visit.

Some Australian cattle herders drive huge herds of cattle for long distances across the outback. Many Aborigines work as cattle herders. They know the land and are able to find water holes in the dry outback.

Children living in the outback are often many miles from the nearest school. This tutor and student are working in a bus that's been turned into a classroom. They can use the computers to talk with teachers and other students miles away.

Rugby football is the most popular sport in New Zealand. Most villages, towns, and districts have their own teams. The national rugby team represents New Zealand in games against other countries. The team is called the All Blacks because the players wear black jerseys and shorts.

All these people live in Australia, New Zealand, and the Pacific Islands.

Many Australians are descended from British settlers. Old-style celebrations, like this one near the Sydney Opera House, take place each year to mark Australia Day.

The people of the Polynesian Islands spend most of their time at sea, fishing and trading with other islands. They have become skillful canoeists.

213

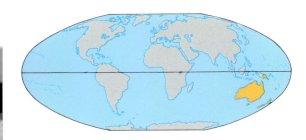

The cities

Most of the large towns and cities of Australia and New Zealand lie along the coast. The climate here is more comfortable than in the hot, dry areas of central Australia or in the cooler mountain areas of New Zealand's North and South islands. Because there is warm sunshine for most of the summer, Australians spend a lot of time out of doors. Cities and towns along the coast often have large sports centers and sheltered bays where all kinds of water sports take place. During the long, hot summers, the beaches near big cities, such as Sydney and Melbourne, get very crowded, and the harbors are filled with yachts.

Vacationers from all over the world visit Fiji and the other island countries. As a result, small towns are growing fast. Even so, the capital of an island country may be no larger than a small town elsewhere.

Sydney is the largest city in Australia. Its huge harbor shelters ships and boats of all sizes, and the nearby beaches are some of the best in the world. Among Sydney's famous landmarks are the Harbor Bridge and the Opera House. ⇓

Alice Springs is an important town that is almost in the middle of Australia and far from any other city. Road and rail traffic link Alice Springs to other cities, and many airplanes stop there during cross-country flights. ⇒

⇑
Canberra is the capital of Australia. The building of the capital began in 1913. The city has been carefully planned, with many parks, wide streets, and an artificial lake. Canberra contains many important modern buildings, including a Parliament House.

Auckland is the largest city on New Zealand's North Island. It is also the country's major seaport, built on a narrow strip of land between two harbors. Many of the country's dairy products and wool are exported from Auckland. The Skytower is New Zealand's tallest building. ⇓

⇑
Fiji is a country made up of more than 800 islands scattered in the South Pacific Ocean. The capital city of Fiji is **Suva.** Suva is a large resort where tourists arrive by ship or yacht. It is also an important port for shipping local products such as sugar, copra, and coconut oil.

Along the Great Barrier Reef

The helicopter rises from Gladstone on the coast of Queensland in Australia and heads out to sea. It is carrying two scientists to the Great Barrier Reef.

This huge reef is really a great chain of separate coral reefs and islands that are scattered for some 1,240 miles (2,000 km) along part of Australia's northeast coast. From the cockpit of the helicopter, the edge of the reef is marked by a line of white surf where the waves of the blue Pacific break on the sharp wall of coral.

The helicopter soon lands on Heron Island on a beach of dazzling white sand, shaded inland by palm trees. But the scientists are here to explore the underwater regions of this coral island. Many kinds of coral grow here—some pink, some yellow, bright blue, or orange. It is like a great underwater garden.

Cairns

Dunk Island

Hook Reef

Heron Island

Gladstone

Coral reefs are home to thousands of fish.

216

The fish of the reef have many ways of protecting themselves. Most are brightly colored. The colors scare off enemies or help the fish to hide among the brilliant coral. Some attack with poisonous spines or sharp teeth.

The next day, the scientists board a small outboard dinghy to continue their journey along the reef. Wearing snorkels and masks, they drop overboard to explore the coral and the thousands of different plants and animals that make their homes just below the surface of the water. They find a blue starfish and bright cowrie shells among the green turtle grass. The divers turn to avoid a mass of floating jellyfish, and suddenly see what they are hunting for—a crown of thorns starfish feeding on the coral. These starfish are the reef's most dangerous enemies. They are almost indestructible, and scientists are still seeking ways to keep them from damaging the reef.

Coral is formed by tiny sea animals called polyps. When the animals die, they leave behind their limestone skeletons. These form the barriers and ridges in the sea known as coral reefs. As millions of polyps grow and die, the coral formations become larger and larger.

Some days later, the scientists reach Hook Reef. Around the island, the sea is dotted with small boats and divers. Some of the islands, such as Hook, are tourist centers.

The journey from Hook Reef to Dunk Island is by boat. The scientists want to observe the seabirds that make their homes on the reef. Thousands of terns build their nests on Beaver Cay, and the red-tailed tropicbird displays its long tail feathers overhead.

Finally, the boat arrives in Cairns, a bustling city on the coast. Cairns developed because it faced one of the two main shipping channels through the reef. Elsewhere, only a few skilled fishermen and sailors can find a safe way through these shallow waters. Over hundreds of thousands of years, the jagged coral has built itself into a true barrier.

217

Welcome to North America

Grizzly bears roam wild in the Rocky Mountains.

Equator

The Golden Gate Bridge, in San Francisco, is one of the world's longest suspension bridges.

Baseball is one of the most popular sports in the United States.

The Grand Canyon has been carved out of the rock by the Colorado River.

North America is the third largest continent in the world. It stretches from the Arctic in the north to the warm tropics in the south.

North America has some spectacular landscapes. The Great Lakes form part of the border between Canada and the United States, the two large countries of this region. The Grand Canyon is a famous attraction in the southwestern United States. A beautiful waterfall, Niagara Falls, is on the border between the United States and Canada. North America is a region of exciting contrasts. Hot deserts stretch across the southwestern part of North America, but parts of Alaska and the far northern part of Canada are frozen wastes. Large areas of North America have few people, and in such places wild animals roam freely. The mountain forests of the north are home to the moose and grizzly bear, while alligators wallow in the swamps of the south.

Most North Americans live and work in or near cities. The largest cities are so crowded that buildings are often dozens of stories high. New York City, Chicago, and Toronto are famous for their towering skyscrapers.

Many forests provide timber.

Mexico City, the capital of Mexico, is one of the largest cities in the world.

219

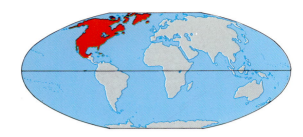

The countries

North America is a huge area of land surrounded by three vast oceans, the Atlantic Ocean, the Pacific Ocean, and the Arctic Ocean. The southern border of Mexico joins North America to its nearest neighbor, Central America. Only a narrow channel of water separates the west coast of the state of Alaska from Russia.

Canada, the United States of America, and Mexico are countries in North America. The territories are Greenland (a province of Denmark), Bermuda (a British dependency), and Saint Pierre et Miquelon (two French islands).

The United States plays an important part in international affairs. It uses its wealth to help poorer nations. The country also spends vast amounts of money on space exploration.

The history

Before the first European settlers arrived in North America, most of the people were hunters who lived very simple lives. They were called Indians by the settlers. In Alaska, northern Canada, and Greenland lived people now known as Inuit.

Christopher Columbus reached North America in 1492. The first settlers from Europe arrived later. As time passed, the settlers explored farther and farther west across this vast land.

At first Great Britain, Spain, the Netherlands, and France each claimed land in parts of North America. But in 1776, 13 British colonies declared themselves an independent republic called the United States of America. Mexico and Canada became independent in the 1800's.

Immigrants and refugees from all over the world come to live and work in the United States and Canada. They have helped to make North America a major power in the world.

The government

The United States is made up of fifty states and the District of Columbia. The district is a piece of land set aside for the nation's capital, Washington, D.C.

The president is the head of state and is elected by the people to serve for four years. But new laws cannot be passed or taxes raised without the approval of the Congress, a body of representatives elected from each state.

Queen Elizabeth of Britain is also the queen of Canada. However, the country is an independent nation, governed by a prime minister and a parliament elected by the people.

Mexico is also a republic, with an elected president and representatives.

The Statue of Liberty is a symbol of freedom.

Canada

Mexico

United States of America

Arctic Ocean

Great Bear Lake

Yukon

Mackenzie

Great Slave Lake

GREENLAND

Hudson Bay

CANADA

Vancouver

Calgary

Lake Winnipeg

Quebec

Montreal

Ottawa

Toronto

St. Lawrence

SAINT PIERRE ET MIQUELON

Pacific Ocean

Great Lakes

Detroit

Missouri

Chicago

Atlantic Ocean

Great Salt Lake

UNITED STATES OF AMERICA

New York City

Philadelphia

Washington D.C.

San Francisco

Los Angeles

BERMUDA

Rio Grande

Houston

Mississippi

MEXICO

Gulf of Mexico

Mexico City

The wealth

The United States and Canada are two of the wealthiest countries in the world. They have almost all the farmland and natural resources they need for their own use. These countries also have skilled workers, very modern machinery, and advanced technology. They use their natural resources to heat their homes and make food and goods.

Facts about North America

There are three independent countries in the region.
Area: 9,064,629 square miles (23,477,277 sq. km).
Population: About 425,392,000.
Largest country: Canada.

Highest mountain: Mt. McKinley, in Alaska, is 20,320 feet (6,194 m) high.
Longest river: The Missouri, in the United States, is 2,540 miles (4,090 km) long.

Looking at the land

North America has a magnificent landscape with long mountain ranges, huge plains, hot deserts in the southwest, and frozen lowlands in the north. A traveler going from north to south, or east to west, will pass through a land of amazing contrasts—through both hot and cold lands and through both mountainous and flat lands.

The North American landscape also offers some world-famous attractions, such as the geyser, Old Faithful. Geysers are underground springs of hot water. A wisp of white steam drifts up from a hole in the rock. Suddenly, there is a gushing sound, and a column of extremely hot water shoots up into the sky. The fountain of steam and water from Old Faithful jets almost 100 feet (30 m) into the air. Then the fountain drops down until there is just a gurgle of water bubbling out of the hole in the ground. Old Faithful is in Yellowstone National Park, in the United States. The geyser may spout more than twenty times a day.

Popocatépetl is an active volcano. From time to time it throws out clouds of gases and steam. It is one of several volcanoes in the high central plain of Mexico. Mexico also has many earthquakes.

The **Grand Canyon** is the world's biggest gorge. It is a deep valley that has been worn down by the Colorado River. In some places the canyon is almost a mile (1.6 km) deep. The walls of the canyon consist of different types of rock and vary in color. The Grand Canyon is part of a national park.

Old Faithful is the name of the most famous geyser in Yellowstone National Park. The park has many natural wonders. It is a popular tourist attraction.

The **Rocky Mountains** form the largest mountain range in North America. They stretch from north to south for more than 3,000 miles (4,800 km) in the western part of North America. There's a long way to go after crossing the Rockies before you reach the west coast of the U.S. Some mountain peaks are covered with snow. On the mountain slopes there are forests of evergreen trees.

Pacific Ocean

Rocky Mountains

Appalachian Mountains

Old Faithful

Niagara Falls

Great Plains

Grand Canyon

Colorado

Popocatépetl

Between the Appalachian Mountains and the Rocky Mountains are the **Great Plains.** They stretch for great distances. Once they were prairies. Now they are covered by farms.

Niagara Falls, one of North America's great natural wonders, forms part of the border between the U.S. and Canada. Here, the Niagara River falls 167 feet (51 m), making a spectacular waterfall.

The plants

Huge evergreen trees grow in California's high forest region. Here are the massive coast redwoods, some of the world's tallest trees. They can soar as high as 260 feet (80 m). Beside the redwoods stand other huge evergreens, such as the Douglas fir. Smaller cypress trees grow below. In forest clearings are tangles of lupines, ferns, and azaleas.

Tall evergreen trees grow along North America's West Coast from California to the slopes of the Rocky Mountains. Evergreen forests cover much of cold northern Canada. Flowering goldenrod turns the fields yellow in summer and autumn. The central prairies are wide, flat grasslands with few trees. Swamp trees and flowers grow in the warm, wet Everglades of southern Florida. And in the dry desert areas of America's Southwest, spiky cactuses thrive.

wheat grass   goldenrod

Kentucky bluegrass

Prairie
The flat prairies, where vast herds of bison once roamed, are carpeted with grasses. Among them are buffalo grass, wheat grass, and Kentucky bluegrass. Sage grows with the grass, but it is uprooted by prairie dogs. They don't like its taste.

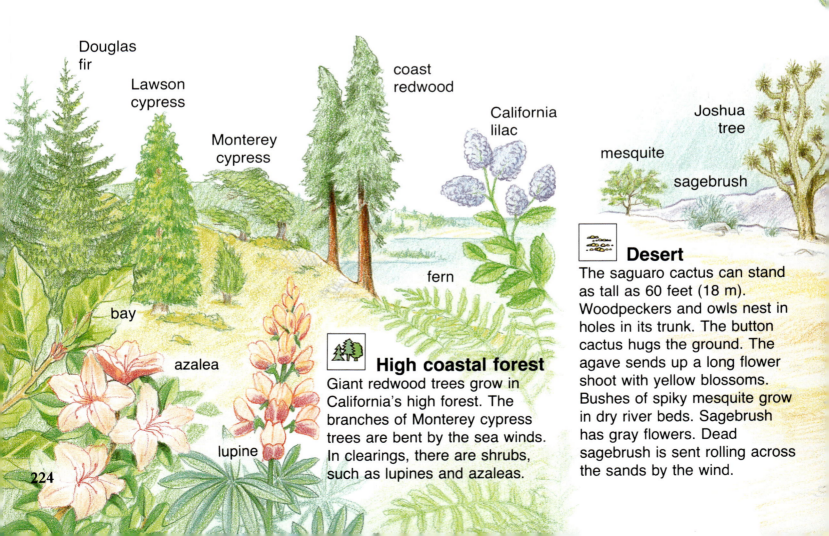

Douglas fir

Lawson cypress

Monterey cypress

coast redwood

California lilac

Joshua tree

mesquite

sagebrush

fern

bay

azalea

lupine

High coastal forest
Giant redwood trees grow in California's high forest. The branches of Monterey cypress trees are bent by the sea winds. In clearings, there are shrubs, such as lupines and azaleas.

Desert
The saguaro cactus can stand as tall as 60 feet (18 m). Woodpeckers and owls nest in holes in its trunk. The button cactus hugs the ground. The agave sends up a long flower shoot with yellow blossoms. Bushes of spiky mesquite grow in dry river beds. Sagebrush has gray flowers. Dead sagebrush is sent rolling across the sands by the wind.

224

spruce

silver fir

white pine

juniper

cranberry

lodgepole pine

Northern forest

Many different trees form the dark-green conifer forests of the north. White, red, and black spruce grow here. They have long brown cones. So does silver fir. Lodgepole pine has sharp spines on its cones. In boggy areas cotton grass thrusts up its fluffy, white seed heads. Cranberry creeps over the ground. It has pink flowers and red berries.

cotton grass

sage

buffalo grass

swamp cypress

saguaro

Spanish moss

trumpet creeper

Florida Everglades

The tall swamp cypress can grow in the water. Spanish moss hangs from its branches. Red iris grows in the mud and has large flowers. Pickerel weed has arrow-shaped leaves and purple flowers. On the banks grows a pink orchid called snakemouth flower. Trumpet creeper climbs on shrubs and trees.

sedge grass

pickerel weed

button cactus

red Iris

agave

snakemouth flower

225

The animals

There are great, cold evergreen forests in the north of the continent. The beaver, one of the biggest rodents in the world, lives here. Beavers are famous for changing the landscape around them. With their strong teeth, they cut down trees to make dams across streams. These dams create ponds in which the beavers build their homes of branches. Grizzly bears also live in the cold forests. Grizzlies are large bears with long, curved claws. They eat fruits, honey, berries, and small animals. And they fish for salmon in the icy rivers. Many of the animals living in this part of North America, such as beavers and grizzlies, have thick coats to keep them warm throughout the long winters. The Canadian lynx has furry feet that help it stalk its prey silently over the snow.

Farther south, there are warmer habitats. Colorful snakes live in the desert areas, along with rabbits and bobcats. In the far southeastern corner of the United States lie the Florida Everglades. Here, many kinds of water birds fish among the reeds, and alligators bask in the sun.

gray squirrel

grizzly bear

salmon

Northern forest

In the spruce and pine forests of the north, gray timber wolves hunt in packs, chasing moose and caribou. Mink hunt birds and fish in the cold streams, and beavers build their homes, called lodges. Grizzlies are large bears. Their fur is brown, streaked with gray hairs. They may be dangerous, but usually they only attack if threatened.

bighorn

marmot

bison

coyote

pronghorn antelope

jack rabbit

prairie dog

mule deer

puma

Prairie

Giant bison used to roam the prairies. Now most of them live in special parks. Coyotes hunt for small animals, such as jack rabbits. In some parts, the ground is full of holes. These are the burrows of small rodents called prairie dogs.

Rocky Mountains

High in the Rockies, there are green pastures where the marmot is putting on fat, ready to sleep all winter. Mule deer move downhill as the weather gets cold. They are hunted by the sleek puma.

blue jay

mink

moose

gray timber wolf

caribou

snowshoe hare

lynx

beaver

gallinule

long-nosed bat

turtle

bobcat

blue heron

jack rabbit

white egret

coral snake

everglade kite

Desert

Jack rabbits rest in the shade, ready to feed at sunset. The bobcat hunts them at night. Long-nosed bats feed on nectar from the desert flowers. Coral snakes are found in this region. They are brilliantly colored—and very poisonous.

Florida Everglades

Alligators, turtles, and fishing birds live in this swampy area.

alligator

Growing and making

The forester takes a small seedling from a bag. It is only a few inches high, but it has a good root and its waxy needles are firm and healthy. The seedling is placed in the top of the planting gun, and with one quick push, it is driven down into the soft soil of the forest clearing. It will grow into a fine pine tree—although that will take twenty or thirty years! Huge areas of the United States and Canada are covered by forests. Some of these are natural forests, and some are planted with special kinds of trees needed to make wood products, such as lumber and paper. New trees are planted as the old ones are cut down.

The warm climate of much of North America is good for growing timber, as well as soybeans and grain crops, such as wheat and corn. Mining is also important, and many metals are used to build cars and trucks. North America is very advanced in science and technology.

Look for these symbols on the map:

🌾	wheat
🌽	corn
🐄	cattle
🥛	dairy products
🍑	fruits
🐚	silk
🪈	tobacco
🌲	timber
🫘	soybeans
⛽	oil
🔥	natural gas
🧲	iron ore
🟨	gold
🏭	industry
💻	computers

Forestry in the U.S.
Foresters plant seedlings in early spring. They use machines called planting guns.

Oil Production in the U.S.
The United States is one of the world's leading producers and refiners of oil. Holes are drilled into the ground through layers of rock to find pools of oil, which is then pumped up to the surface.

Corn growing in Mexico

Large amounts of corn are grown in Mexico. The corn is planted in rows and can grow up to ten feet (3 m) high. The cobs of corn have large, yellow grains. They are eaten whole or dried and ground into flour. The grain is also squeezed to get corn oil.

Car manufacturing in the U.S.

The U.S. is one of the world's leading car manufacturers. Many people work in the factories, but there are also robots to do jobs on the assembly line.

Computer making in the U.S.

The world's largest concentration of computer industries is found in California. Here, silicon chips are manufactured.

People and how they live

Vacations in the country are popular in North America, especially with people who live in the large cities and towns. In the rural areas, the pace of life is slower and more relaxing. People can enjoy the peace and quiet and get away from the bustle of city life. Many Americans go camping or hiking near lakes or in the mountains.

Many people in North America earn good wages and have a lot of free time. Sports are a very popular pastime. Baseball, basketball, football, and ice hockey are all favorite sports. Baseball is so popular in the United States that it is often called the national pastime. There are organized baseball teams for every age group from small children to adults.

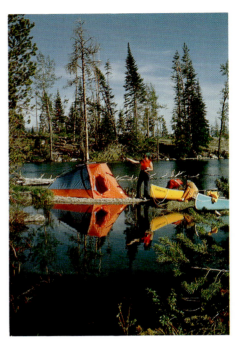

There are many beautiful areas in North America that are used as national parks. In these places, people can relax and enjoy the outdoor life. Camping in the forests and mountains and on the shores of lakes is a favorite activity.

All these people live in North America.

230

A rodeo is a tough contest for riders and cowhands. Thousands of rodeos are held each year in the American West. The most exciting event is the bareback bronco riding. The rider must stay on a bucking horse for eight seconds.

You can find almost any kind of food from anywhere in the world in the cities of North America. Fast food shops sell hamburgers and hot dogs. Italian restaurants sell pasta and pizzas. Chinese restaurants serve noodles and fried rice. And ice-cream parlors and coffee shops are common.

Native Americans have lived in North America since prehistoric times. Land has been set aside as reservations for the Native Americans to live on. The children often go to special schools. Many Navaho people earn their living by selling traditional blankets and jewelry to tourists.

Football is one of America's favorite sports. Players wear pads and helmets as they try to stop the other team from scoring.

231

The cities

North America has many cities, and more than two-thirds of the people live in cities. New York is the largest city in the United States. It is also one of the most famous cities in the world. It is full of buildings and monuments, such as the Empire State Building and the Statue of Liberty. There are many skyscrapers, all built so closely together that they block out the sunlight for smaller buildings below.

There are many cities in North America where millions of people crowd into skyscraper homes and offices. Away from the city centers there are neighborhoods of older houses. Many recent immigrants to North America live in such neighborhood communities. Buildings aren't so high on the edges of the big cities. Here, one- or two-story houses stretch into the distance.

↑
The busy city of **San Francisco** has some of the world's steepest streets. One part of the city is called Chinatown. The shops there are built in Chinese style, with upturned roofs.

The big cities of North America are full of bustle, color, and noise. **New York City's** nickname is the Big Apple. More than twenty million people live in New York City and its suburbs. Land is scarce, so many buildings are tall. People live and work in these towering skyscrapers.
↓

⇑

Calgary is an important Canadian city with many modern buildings. The Olympic Saddledome is an indoor sports arena, which was built for the 1988 Winter Olympic Games. Another city landmark is the red and white Calgary Tower. At its top are an observation deck and a restaurant.

Quebec City lies on the St. Lawrence River and is an important port. The old part of the city looks like a French town, with its old stone houses, narrow cobbled streets, and many churches. A famous old hotel, the Château Frontenac, overlooks the river. ⇓

⇑

Mexico City is the capital of Mexico. The country was ruled by the Spanish for 300 years and it has many Spanish-style buildings. As in many other Mexican cities, the capital's main buildings stand around wide plazas, or squares. There are often colorful markets.

233

Across North America by bus

The luggage is loaded, everyone has found a seat, and the bus is ready to leave. For the passengers, this is the start of a wonderful ride across North America. It begins on the West Coast in the bus terminal at Los Angeles. It will end in three weeks in New York City, on the East Coast. The passengers have a special ticket that will allow them to change buses along the way. They will be able to get off whenever they want to stop and see the sights and then continue their journey on the next bus that comes along.

After the mountain forests of the California coast are left behind, the bus soon enters the vast wasteland of the Mojave Desert.

The bus soon reaches one of the world's most spectacular sights, the Grand Canyon in Arizona. Everyone wants to watch the sunset here, when the rocks are transformed into a multicolored display.

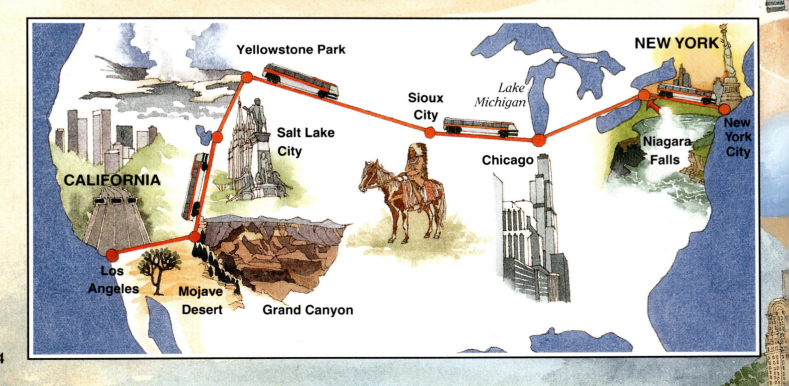

Yellowstone Park

NEW YORK

Salt Lake City

Sioux City

Lake Michigan

CALIFORNIA

Chicago

Niagara Falls

New York City

Los Angeles

Mojave Desert

Grand Canyon

Salt Lake City, in the state of Utah, is a favorite stop for bus tourists. This modern center, set among mountains and deserts, was founded many years ago by a group of Mormon settlers who wanted freedom to practice their religion. At one time, Native Americans wandered over the northern plains of America. One group, the Sioux, farmed and hunted buffalo, but they were especially famous for their bravery and fighting skills. Sioux City, in Iowa, is named after the Sioux people. Today, most Sioux live on reservations, where many of them farm or raise cattle.

Later, the bus passes near Yellowstone National Park, where there are waterfalls, hot pools, and geysers that spurt steam high into the air. Bear and bison roam freely in the park.

Some Native Americans wear their traditional clothes for tourists.

Chicago is famous for its spectacular skyscrapers.

Chicago has many famous buildings, including the Sears Tower, one of the tallest buildings in the world. This busy city stands on the southernmost tip of Lake Michigan, one of North America's five Great Lakes. Many people board the bus here to travel northeast toward Canada.

On the United States-Canadian border, the passengers leave the bus to board a sightseeing steamer that sails right into the spray of the mighty, thundering Niagara Falls.

The last ride takes the passengers into New York City. The city's towering buildings are almost as breathtaking as some of the natural wonders the tourists have seen along the way.

235

Welcome to Central America and the Caribbean Islands

Many kinds of tropical fruits are grown throughout the Caribbean Islands.

Tourists visit the warm, sandy beaches of the Caribbean Islands.

Equator

Wooden houses line many streets in Antigua.

Calypso music is played by steel bands.

Bananas grown on plantations are sold all over the world.

Central America is a region between Mexico and South America. It is crossed by the Panama Canal, which joins the Atlantic Ocean and the Pacific Ocean. It is one of the busiest waterways in the world. To the east, in the Caribbean Sea, are thousands of islands, both large and small. The largest of the islands is Cuba, where Spanish is spoken. The largest English-speaking island is Jamaica in the West Indies. Some of these islands are made of coral; others are mountainous, volcanic islands.

The weather here is hot and humid, for the region lies just south of the Tropic of Cancer. Hurricanes often occur, but the climate is ideal for growing sugarcane and tobacco, as well as bananas and other tropical fruits. Brightly colored birds live on the islands and along the coasts, and the rain forests are alive with monkeys and other creatures.

Ships use the Panama Canal to avoid a long journey around the tip of South America.

In Guatemala, people sell their crops at village markets.

237

The countries

Central America forms the western part of this region. There are seven countries in the region. These are Belize, Costa Rica, El Salvador, Guatemala, Honduras, Nicaragua, and Panama. To the north of Guatemala and Belize is Mexico. To the south of Panama is South America. The Pacific Ocean lies to the west, and the Caribbean Sea, which is part of the Atlantic Ocean, is to the east.

The eastern rim of the region is formed by a chain of islands called the West Indies. These islands form three main groups. These are the Bahamas, the Greater Antilles, and the Lesser Antilles. The Caribbean Sea lies between these islands and Central America.

Antigua and Barbuda

Bahamas

Barbados

Belize

Costa Rica

Cuba

The history

More than 2,000 years ago, many groups of American Indians lived in Central America. One group, the Maya, were skilled engineers and builders. The ruins of their great temples and cities can still be seen.

Spanish explorers were the first Europeans to discover this area. For about 300 years, Spain ruled over most of Central America. Many of the islands in the Caribbean were later seized from Spain by other European countries, such as France, Britain, and the Netherlands.

In 1914, a canal was dug across Panama between the Atlantic and Pacific oceans. This meant that ships could sail through the canal from one ocean to the other instead of making the long voyage around the tip of South America. The canal was built by the United States and is run by Panama.

The Panama Canal is an important waterway that cuts across Central America.

Dominica

Dominican Republic

El Salvador

Grenada

Guatemala

Haiti

Honduras

Jamaica

Nicaragua

Panama

St. Kitts and Nevis

St. Lucia

St. Vincent and the Grenadines

Trinidad and Tobago

Gulf of Mexico

BELIZE

GUATEMALA
Lake Atitlán
Guatemala City

HONDURAS
Tegucigalpa

EL SALVADOR

NICARA
Manag

Pacific Ocean

San J

C

The government

Six of the countries of Central America are republics. Only Belize is a monarchy. Its head of state is Queen Elizabeth II of Great Britain.

In the past, many Central American countries have been ruled by military leaders who were not elected by the people. Today, there are clashes between the people, and even civil wars in some countries. This brings suffering to everyone and destroys the wealth of these countries.

Most of the islands of the Caribbean are independent and rule themselves. However, some are still partly ruled by France, the Netherlands, or Great Britain.

The wealth

In the past, bananas, coffee, and sugar cane brought great wealth to Central America. But then the prices of these crops began to fall. More crops had to be produced to earn the same money. The countries of Central America also borrowed large amounts of money from Europe and the United States to pay for the fuel they needed. Today, they do not earn enough money to repay these debts easily.

Another problem in this area is that the population is growing too quickly. This means that there are not enough jobs for everyone, and many people are very poor. In some countries, new industries, such as tourism, are being developed to provide more jobs.

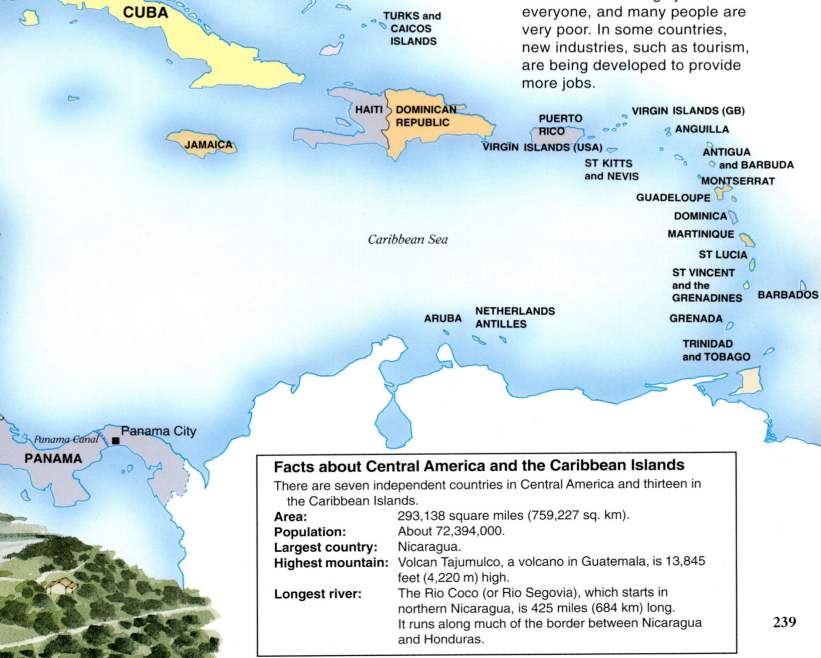

Havana

BAHAMAS

Atlantic Ocean

CUBA

TURKS and CAICOS ISLANDS

JAMAICA

HAITI DOMINICAN REPUBLIC

PUERTO RICO

VIRGIN ISLANDS (USA)

VIRGIN ISLANDS (GB)

ANGUILLA

ST KITTS and NEVIS

ANTIGUA and BARBUDA

MONTSERRAT

GUADELOUPE

DOMINICA

MARTINIQUE

ST LUCIA

ST VINCENT and the GRENADINES

BARBADOS

Caribbean Sea

ARUBA NETHERLANDS ANTILLES

GRENADA

TRINIDAD and TOBAGO

Panama Canal Panama City

PANAMA

Facts about Central America and the Caribbean Islands

There are seven independent countries in Central America and thirteen in the Caribbean Islands.

Area:	293,138 square miles (759,227 sq. km).
Population:	About 72,394,000.
Largest country:	Nicaragua.
Highest mountain:	Volcan Tajumulco, a volcano in Guatemala, is 13,845 feet (4,220 m) high.
Longest river:	The Rio Coco (or Rio Segovia), which starts in northern Nicaragua, is 425 miles (684 km) long. It runs along much of the border between Nicaragua and Honduras.

239

Looking at the land

The clear, blue Caribbean Sea stretches between the white, sandy beaches of the West Indies and the coasts of Central America. Winds that blow softly from the northeast, gentle tides, and air free of pollution and fog make this region especially beautiful. Just below the surface of the warm waters are glistening coral reefs, alive with colorful fish. Here and there, the coral is marked with nature trails for divers and swimmers to follow.

Many islands in the West Indies are made of coral. Others were once volcanoes that built upward from the seabed. Earthquakes and volcanic eruptions still occur in this region, causing much damage and making many people homeless. However, the rich volcanic soil is very fertile farmland.

East of the mountains of **Nicaragua** are some of the largest plains in Central America. These flat areas are crossed by many rivers. Most of the rivers flow into the Caribbean Sea.

Lake Atitlán

Nicaragua

Lake Atitlán is a large lake in the highlands of Central America. Around the lake are volcanoes and many hot springs. Hot springs on the lake bed heat the water. Hot currents containing dissolved minerals change the color of the lake water from blues to greens.

Magnificent coral reefs run along the coast of **Barbados.** Much of this island is made of coral. On the beaches, the sea has worn the coral into fine pink and white sand.

Mont Pelée is an active volcano on the French island of Martinique. It erupted in 1902. White-hot volcanic ash and scorching steam swept down the slopes of the volcano.

Caribbean Sea

Mont Pelée

St Lucia

Barbados

Two oddly shaped mountains rise from the sea on the coast of **Saint Lucia.** They are called the Gros Piton, which is French for Big Peak, and the Petit Piton, or Little Peak. They were formed long ago by hot, liquid rock that welled up inside the cones of volcanoes. The sides of the volcanoes were later worn away by the wind and rain. Now, only these two tall rocky peaks remain.

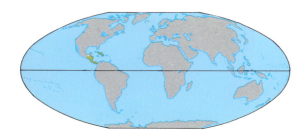

Plants and animals

beefsteak
Heliconia

trumpet tree

ruby-throated
hummingbird

Poinsettia

Each dawn, the animals of the tropical rain forest awake to the strange call of the howler monkeys. High among the branches of the tallest trees, birds ruffle their bright feathers and whistle and squawk. The forest is full of noise and color. Many rare and beautiful flowers grow high in the trees, their roots drinking in moisture from the damp air. Mosses and ferns cover the branches with a layer of soft green.

On the forest floor below, it is dark. Hardly any sunlight finds its way down through the thick layers of leaves. Very few plants can grow in this gloom.

Many of the animals and birds of the forests of Central America, such as the quetzal, are becoming very rare. Other unusual creatures live in the islands of the West Indies. Some of them are found nowhere else in the world.

Forest riverbank

Tapirs live along the riverbanks in Central America. They spend much time in the water and feed on plants. The two-toed sloth moves very slowly through the trees, feeding on leaves. The tayra is much more active, hunting mice and squirrels. Tiny hummingbirds visit flowers in search of nectar.

tree porcupine

four-eyed
opossum

bromeliad

kinkajou

howler
monkey

Rain Forest

High up in the tree branches, rare and colorful orchids grow. Flowering bromeliads hold little pools of water in their cupped leaves. The rain forest animals are colorful too. A bird called the quetzel has bright green and red feathers. At night, the kinkajou comes out. It can hang by its tail to reach the fruits of wild fig and avocado trees.

moss

fern

orchid

quetzal

leopard
frog

margay

two-toed sloth

tayra

scarlet ibis

tropicbird

frigate bird

coconut palm

mangrove

West Indian manatee

Baird's tapir

robber crab

Island coasts

Coconut palms line the coasts of many West Indian islands. Robber crabs climb the palms and snip off coconuts. Scarlet ibises search the mud for worms. In the water, fat, slow manatees feed on underwater plants. Tropicbirds and frigate birds glide over the sea looking for fish.

Jamaican hutia

St. Lucia parrot

St. Vincent parrot

rhinoceros iguana

Caribbean Islands

Huge lizards called rhinoceros iguanas live on some of the islands. The Jamaican hutia lives only in Jamaica. It feeds on the plants of the forests and hills. Several islands have birds that are found nowhere else, like the St. Vincent parrot and the St. Lucia parrot.

243

Growing and making

The cane cutters straighten up and wipe sweat from their foreheads. They sweat heavily in the burning sun. The tall sugar cane stands over fifteen feet (5 m) high. They bend again and swing their heavy, sharp machetes low against the sugar cane stalks. They strip off the leaves and lop the tops from the stalks. The cut stalks lie in stacks to wait for the bullock cart to collect them. Where the land is flat, machines sometimes do the cutting, but people have to do it on the slopes and rough ground.

The countries of Central America depend on growing sugar cane, coffee, and tobacco. There is drilling for oil, too. Ships sail the Caribbean, carrying crops and oil from the region to other countries. The tourist industry is important in the Caribbean, and many hotels, restaurants, and night clubs have been built for visitors.

Cutting sugar cane in Central America

On hilly ground, people cut the sugar cane. Much of the sugar we eat is made by crushing the sweet juice out of the stalk.

Look for all these symbols on the map:

rice		tobacco		
corn		timber		
cattle		fishing		
fruits		oil		
sugar		bauxite		
coffee		industry		
bananas				

Coffee growing in Central America

Coffee is grown on the huge plantations of El Salvador, Guatemala, and Costa Rica. Many workers live on the plantations all year round, caring for the coffee plants and harvesting the red coffee berries.

Oil industry in Trinidad

Trinidad has several large oil fields and two big refineries to turn the oil into gasoline and diesel fuel. Trinidad's Pitch Lake was formed over thousands of years as unrefined, or crude, oil seeped out of the ground into the lake. The lake is black and sticky. The sludgy mixture can be used as asphalt for paving roads.

Tourist industry in the Caribbean

Millions of tourists come to the islands of the Caribbean every year to swim or sunbathe on the beautiful beaches. They can also go fishing, snorkeling, or scuba diving.

Tobacco growing in Cuba

Cuban tobacco is used to make the famous Havana cigars. The tobacco plants grow up to ten feet (3 m) high. The tops of the plants are taken off to stop flowers from growing. About twenty large, sticky leaves grow. These are picked, dried, and shredded to make tobacco.

245

People and cities

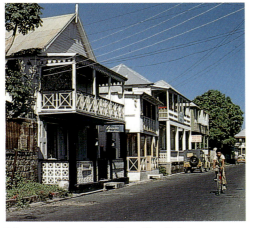

Most of the people of Central America live in the high regions, where they work on the land. Many are very poor and find it hard to earn a living. Today, many people are moving to the cities to look for jobs, better schools for their children, and health care for their families.

Many different groups of people live in the region. They are mainly descended from the Africans and Spaniards who came to Central America hundreds of years ago. There are also many Indians in the region. In Guatemala, you can hear a variety of Indian languages.

Each group of people has its own traditions and customs. Music is important in the Caribbean Islands, the home of lively reggae and calypso songs. The wide variety of life styles in Central America can be seen in the city streets, in festivals and celebrations, in the colorful clothing—and in the food.

Many houses in the Caribbean Islands are designed with a long veranda. A veranda is a platform built on the front of a house, at ground level or higher levels. It gives shelter from the sun and rain, and it is open to the cool breezes in summer.

All these people live in Central America and the Caribbean Islands.

Handweaving is a traditional Indian craft. Young girls learn at an early age how to spin and weave, using richly colored wools.

246

Guatemala City was almost completely flattened by earthquakes in 1917. Now it has been rebuilt. Guatemala City is the center of Guatemala's industry and coffee trade.

At the Pacific end of the Panama Canal is **Panama City,** the capital of Panama. After the canal was opened in 1914, the city grew very quickly. It is now a modern center of trade and industry, with modern apartment and office buildings lining the coast.

Fruit is an important food for the people of the West Indies. Bananas, lemons, oranges, mangoes, and pineapples are exported throughout the world.

In Jamaica, the music of a steel band often fills the air. Several different kinds of instruments are played, but the strong rhythm of the band is made on the big steel drums. These are empty oil drums, often cut down to make shallower drums. The shallower the drum, the higher the tone, and so a whole range of sounds can be created.

Welcome to South America

Toucans live in the rain forest.

Equator

Llamas are most useful as pack animals. They are sure-footed on steep and narrow mountain trails.

On the slopes of the Andes, farme build terraces for their crops.

South America is the fourth largest continent. It has the longest mountain range and the largest rain forest in the world.

South America is joined to Central America by a narrow strip of land called the Isthmus of Panama. The rest of the continent is shaped like a triangle. The widest part of the continent lies on the equator. The climate here is hot and wet. But the southern tip of South America is in the cold waters of the South Atlantic and South Pacific oceans.

Some areas of South America are still unexplored. The great Amazon rain forest is one of the few places on earth where new kinds of animals and plants can still be discovered.

Many people live in cities and work in offices or industries. Outside the towns and cities, people make a living by raising cattle and sheep, growing crops, or mining oil and minerals.

The Amazon River winds through the tropical rain forest.

Modern buildings dot the skylines of Brazil's major cities.

The Mardi Gras carnival is held each year in Rio de Janeiro.

249

The countries

South America is a vast continent that lies to the south of North America. Between these two huge areas lies a long narrow area called Central America.

There are twelve independent countries in South America. There are also two territories, which are not independent. These are the Falkland Islands, which are governed by Britain, and French Guiana, which is governed by France. In the past, Argentina and Britain fought over ownership of the Falkland Islands.

Brazil is by far the largest country in South America. It covers almost half of this region. Brazil has a larger population than all the other countries of South America combined.

The government

Most of the countries in this region are republics, which rule themselves.

In Brazil, everyone over the age of eighteen can vote to elect the government and the president, who is the head of state. A president is elected to rule for four years. The president may not be elected more than two terms in a row.

The governments of many South American countries are fighting such problems as unemployment and poverty. Many South American countries have borrowed large sums of money from the United States and Europe.

The history

The first people to live in South America were Indians. The most powerful tribe was the Inca. In the 1500's, soldiers from Spain conquered the Inca and claimed their land. Settlers from Portugal also came to South America. These settlers were cruel to the Indians, and many Indians died. Then the settlers brought slaves from Africa. Over the next few hundred years, the settlers grew very rich by trading in crops grown by slaves.

By the early 1800's, most South American countries wanted to rule themselves. Fighting broke out in many countries. Two generals, Simón Bolívar and José de San Martín, helped win independence for several countries, such as Bolivia, Colombia, Ecuador, Peru, and Venezuela. By 1830, most countries were independent.

Simón Bolívar helped win independence for many South American countries.

Argentina

Bolivia

Brazil

Chile

Colombia

Ecuador

Guyana

Paraguay

Peru

Suriname

Uruguay

Venezuela

GALAPAGOS
ISLANDS

Caracas

VENEZUELA

GUYANA

FRENCH
GUIANA

Bogotá

SURINAME

COLOMBIA

Amazon

Amazon

Quito

ECUADOR

BRAZIL

Lima

PERU

Brasília

Lake
Titicaca

La Paz

BOLIVIA

Rio de Janeiro

CHILE

PARAGUAY

São Paulo

ARGENTINA

URUGUAY

Montevideo

Santiago

Buenos Aires

FALKLAND
ISLANDS

The wealth

About one-fourth of the people in South America live in rural areas. Many of these people are poor farmers who work small plots of land. But there are also wealthy landowners who have huge cattle ranches and plantations.

South America has some of the largest deposits of valuable minerals in the world. But most countries do not have the factories they need to process the minerals. In many countries, the governments are encouraging business people to build more factories for making textiles and refining foods, such as sugar. Such factories could bring more employment and wealth to South America.

Facts about South America

There are twelve independent countries in the region.

Area: 6,885,000 square miles (17,832,000 sq. km).

Population: About 360,884,000.

Largest country: Brazil.

Highest mountain: Mount Aconcagua, in the Argentine Andes, is 22,831 feet (6,959 m) high.

Longest river: The Amazon River is 4,000 miles (6,437 km) long.

Looking at the land

The Andes Mountains stretch like a backbone down the western coast of South America. High up in the grassy valleys and on the steep slopes, strong winds constantly blow and heavy rain pours down in torrents. But farmers here must live with greater problems than these. Their huts and crops may be swept away by a landslide during the wettest times, and these ancient mountains are still jolted by volcanoes and earthquakes that destroy whole villages.

There are other rugged areas of the eastern side of the continent, such as the Guiana Highlands and the Brazilian Highlands. But the land is much lower than the Andes.

The chief river of South America is the Amazon. It begins as a stream high in the Andes Mountains, and flows across Brazil to the Atlantic Ocean. The Amazon carries more water than any other river in the world. A thick, green rain forest stretches along most of its length.

The muddy-brown **Amazon** is 4,000 miles (6,437 km) long, and is the second longest river in the world. It carries one-fifth of the running water in the world. At certain times of the year the Amazon floods the surrounding countryside, destroying plants and trees. Thousands of smaller rivers feed into the Amazon.

Lake Titicaca is 12,507 feet (3,812 m) above sea level in the Andes Mountains. The Indians sometimes live on "floating islands" in the lake.

These are not real islands. They are large rafts made of reeds. Reed boats, called totoras, carry people around the lake.

The world's highest waterfall is **Angel Falls** in the Guiana Highlands. It is 3,212 feet (979 m) high. The falls were named after Jimmy Angel, an American. He found the falls while looking for gold.

Lake Maracaibo

Andes Mountains

Angel Falls

Negro

Amazon

Amazon

Xingu

Madeira

São Francisco

Lake Titicaca

Pacific Ocean

Paraguay

Paraná

Atlantic Ocean

Atacama Desert

Andes Mountains

The **Andes** range is the world's longest mountain chain. It stretches thousands of miles (kilometers) from southern Chile to Venezuela. There are many high mountain peaks in the Andes. Many peaks are the cones of volcanoes.

The **Atacama Desert** is a region of sand and gravel that runs along the coasts of Chile and Peru. There are places here where no rainfall has ever been recorded. But in other places, streams flow across the desert. These start in the snow-covered Andes Mountains to the east. The desert is rich in valuable minerals. The Chileans call the desert "The Great North."

The plants

Deep in the rain forest, the air is hot, wet, and still. The forest floor is dark and gloomy, and few plants grow here. Higher up, layers of trees and shrubs form a covering or canopy. And higher still, a thick blanket of leaves makes a great, green roof. A Brazil-nut tree towers to the very top of the canopy. It is one of the tallest trees in the forest. Climbing plants, called lianas, grow around its trunk and branches, with their leaves in the sunlight. High in the branches grow rare orchids and bromeliads.

The rain forest of South America is the largest in the world. The forest trees are always green, and flowers and fruit are produced all year round. Farther south, the land is drier and colder. Grasses and shrubs grow here. In the southern desert area, cactuses survive even the driest conditions. At the southern tip of South America, icy winds blow in from Antarctica during winter. Here, the plants have just a short time to grow before the winter snows arrive.

Victoria water lily

Rain forest

The great rain forest of the Amazon is hot and wet. Trees grow thickly, fighting to reach the sunlight. Many trees, such as the Brazil-nut tree, are covered with lianas, orchids, and brightly colored bromeliads. Vanilla flavoring comes from one kind of orchid. In the rivers grow giant Victoria water lilies.

Plantago sericea

ichu grass

Llaretta

Andes Mountains

The Andes Mountains stretch down the west coast of South America. The high mountain plains are covered with shrubs and grasses, such as ichu grass and llaretta. The highest peaks are bare rock and ice.

254

vanilla
orchid

liana

Brazil-nut tree

bromeliad

Desert

There are many cactuses on the dry eastern slopes of the Andes. Spiky-leaved Tillandsias grow here, too. When rain falls, Nolanas, begonias, and lilies burst into flower.

paper-spine
cactus

desert lily

begonia

Tillandsia

Nolana

pampas grass

prairie
grass

Grassland

The pampas, in central Argentina, is one of South America's grassland areas. The flat plains are covered with tall, dry pampas grass and prairie grass.

255

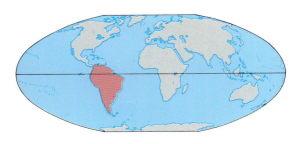

The animals

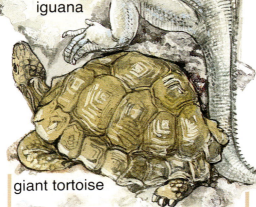

iguana

giant tortoise

As night falls, the rain forest comes alive with rustles, squeaks, and calls. Jaguars move along the banks of streams in search of prey. Huge anacondas silently uncoil, ready for their next meal. And spider monkeys, the acrobats of the monkey world, swing through the trees overhead. They use their long legs and tails to cling to the branches.

Hundreds of different kinds of animals live in the South American rain forest. Brightly colored birds and a huge assortment of insects make their homes among the crowded trees and plants. But in the desert, where there is little food, only a few kinds of animals can survive. The grasslands are home to many small burrowing animals, such as the armadillo. And in South America's high mountain slopes live the chinchilla and the llama, protected from the cold by their thick, warm coats.

Galapagos Islands
The Galapagos Islands lie in the Pacific Ocean. Many interesting animals live here, including marine iguanas, the world's only sea lizards. The giant tortoises are among the largest in the world.

toucan

sloth

anaconda

spider monkey

jaguar

tapir

hummingbird

macaw

Rain forest
The rain forest is home to giant creatures, such as the huge morpho butterfly and the great anaconda. Bird-eating spiders may be three inches (8 cm) long.

blue morpho butterfly

bird-eating spider

capybara

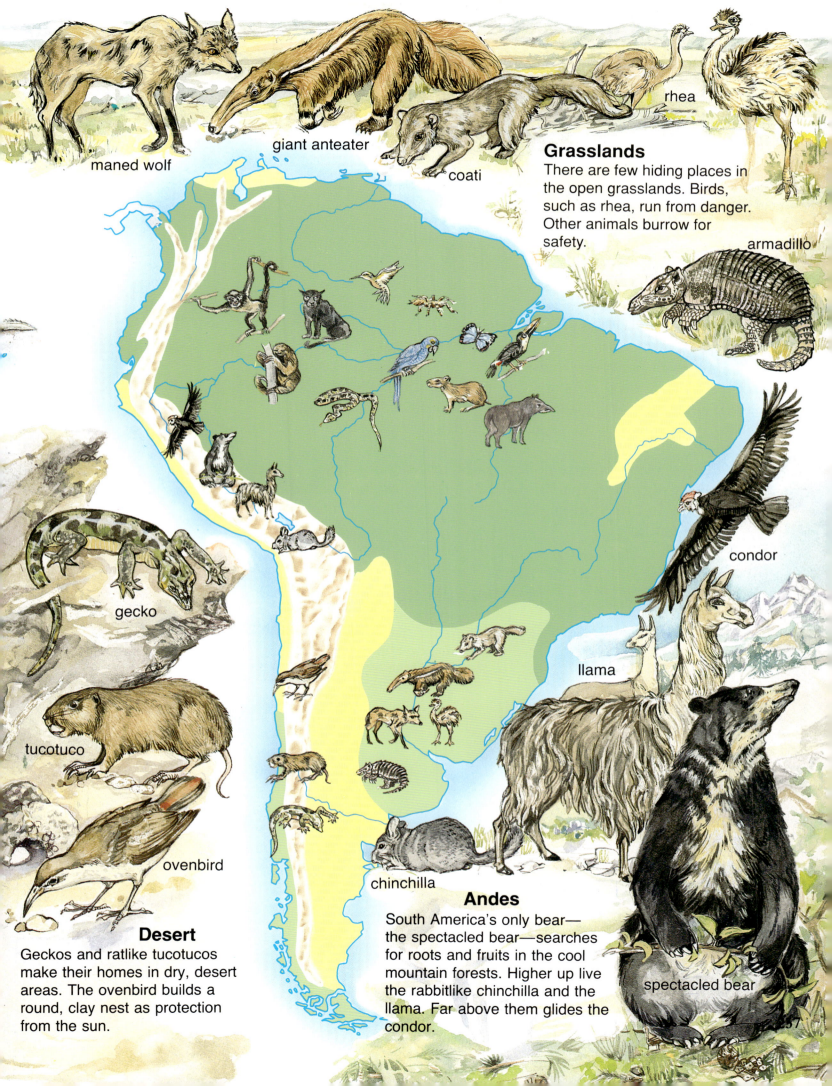

maned wolf

giant anteater

coati

rhea

Grasslands
There are few hiding places in the open grasslands. Birds, such as rhea, run from danger. Other animals burrow for safety.

armadillo

condor

llama

gecko

tucotuco

ovenbird

Desert
Geckos and ratlike tucotucos make their homes in dry, desert areas. The ovenbird builds a round, clay nest as protection from the sun.

chinchilla

Andes
South America's only bear—the spectacled bear—searches for roots and fruits in the cool mountain forests. Higher up live the rabbitlike chinchilla and the llama. Far above them glides the condor.

spectacled bear

Growing and making

Deep in the mine, machines roar and workers shout to each other. The air is hot and dusty. It is hard, dirty work, drilling into the rock under the high mountain slopes of the Andes. But it is worth the trouble. The miners find large deposits of copper and gold in the rock.

The mountains of the west are rich in silver, iron, tin, manganese, and sulfur as well as gold and copper. Another very important natural resource is oil. Venezuela is one of the world's leading oil producers. Oil is also found in Peru, Brazil, Ecuador, and Argentina. Other important industries in South American countries include textiles, leather, cars, and cement.

The large farms produce cotton, coffee, wheat, and beef. The owners of these farms are wealthy. There are many small farmers, too, but they are poor and must work hard just to feed their families.

Mining in South America
Many mines continue to operate underground, but today most mining is done above ground, in large open-pit mines.

Look for these symbols on the map:

- wheat
- cattle
- sheep
- sugar
- cotton
- coffee
- cocoa
- bananas
- timber
- fishing
- soybeans
- oil
- iron ore
- gold
- copper
- industry

Oil industry in Venezuela
Lake Maracaibo in Venezuela is a major oil-producing area. To reach the oil, wells have to be drilled from platforms on the water. Pipelines carry the oil to the coast. From here it is shipped all over the world.

Cacao growing in Brazil
Brazil is one of the world's largest producer of cocoa beans, which grow on the cacao tree.

The tree has bright orange pods, and inside are the cocoa beans from which chocolate is made.

Banana growing in Ecuador
Bananas are grown mainly on plantations near the coast. When they are harvested, they must be carried on mules to the river. Small boats carry the bananas down the river to large banana boats. These boats have cool chambers to keep the fruit from ripening too soon. The banana boats sail all over the world.

Cattle ranching in Argentina
The huge ranches found on the pampas, the grassy plains of Argentina, are called *estancias*. Beef cattle are raised for meat, and the skins are made into leather. The meat is exported in refrigerated ships, or canned as corned beef. Cowboys who herd the cattle are called *gauchos*.

259

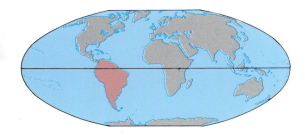

People and how they live

Many of the people of South America are very poor. In the rural areas, most people own small plots of land on which they grow only enough food for their own needs. They must sometimes struggle to support their families. Some people are able to grow extra food to sell at market. Others work for the rich ranch owners who raise cattle on the pampas. Many others move to the cities to try to find jobs.

Today, three-fourths of the South American people live in the cities. Here, some people may find work, as well as a local doctor and schools for the children. But many adults cannot read or write, and they learn about the world by watching television. Wherever they live, people come together to enjoy music and dancing whenever they can. The Indians of the Amazon have a dance for each special occasion. The Peruvian Indians, who live in the high Andes, play on homemade wooden flutes. And each year, in cities, towns, and villages, many carnivals take place to celebrate religious festivals and national holidays.

On the banks of the Amazon River, many houses are built on tall wooden stilts as protection from floods. The people catch turtles and fish and plant crops in the fertile mud left each year by the flood waters.

In La Paz, in Bolivia, there is a large market where local Indians sell flowers, fruit, vegetables, beads, and medicines.

There is a festival every February in Rio de Janeiro, Brazil. Thousands of people parade and dance through the streets, wearing colorful costumes. And crowds gather to watch the festivities.

South American cowboys, called *gauchos,* work on the rolling grasslands of the pampas. They wear hats and heavy riding boots. These gauchos are dressed in their best traditional riding outfits.

The Indians of the Amazon live in the hot, damp rain forest. They wear little clothing. Sometimes the children wear none at all. Often as many as sixty people live together in a family group. They fish, hunt, and grow crops for food. They build their homes from trees.

All these people live in South America.

261

The cities

Most people in South America live in the crowded cities. People have flocked here from rural areas. Unfortunately, they do not always find what they need. Housing is scarce and expensive. The poor people live in buildings made of wood and tin or even cardboard. Some of the poorest people live in the streets or on the beaches.

Most of the large modern cities have been built along the coasts of the Atlantic and Pacific oceans. Towering skyscrapers of concrete and glass rise above the narrow streets. These cities have grown up around bustling ports and harbors. They play an important part in the life of the country, as most products still arrive and leave by sea. In fact, in Buenos Aires, the capital of Argentina, the people are called *porteños,* which means "port dwellers."

⇧
The ancient city of **Machu Picchu** in Peru lay hidden for more than 300 years before it was discovered again in 1911. Machu Picchu was built by the early South American Indians, the Inca. Today the ruined city, with its palaces, terraces, and 3,000 stairs, is an important tourist attraction.

⇦ **Rio de Janeiro** is perched on a shelf of land between the mountains and the sea. A huge statue called *Christ the Redeemer* overlooks the city from atop Corcovado Mountain. The famous Sugar Loaf Mountain rises above the bay. Rio is Brazil's second largest city. More than 10 million people live in the city and its suburbs.

Caracas, the capital of Venezuela, is a city built from oil wealth. It stands in a narrow valley near the coast and has grown quickly. The buildings in Caracas are a mixture of poor shanty houses, grand colonial palaces, and modern skyscrapers. ⤓

Santiago is the capital and largest city of Chile. It is surrounded by mountains and hills. The Andes, the highest mountain range in South America, rise above the city to the east. ⤏

Brasília is the capital of Brazil. Building of the city began in 1956, in an area of wilderness in the center of the country. Brasília was carefully planned and contains some of the world's most modern architecture. The government buildings are especially striking. These unusual buildings are where Brazil's Congress meets. ⤓

263

Journey up the Amazon

The passengers crowd along the rails as the steamer pulls out of the port of Belém into the center of the Pará River. Someone has spotted a water buffalo in the swampy mud close to the bank. The passengers laugh and cheer as two young boys lasso one of the horns and pull the animal onto dry land. They will use the water buffalo to finish the day's plowing on the island of Marajó.

Once past the island, the steamer leaves the Pará River and enters the Amazon. The passengers are traveling up this vast river past Óbidos toward Manaus, a popular tourist center. The Amazon is too wide at many points for people to see the opposite bank. As they travel, they pass other ships carrying cargoes of Amazon products.

At Manaus, the steamer ends its journey. Some passengers stop here to visit the city's Indian museum and the zoo, which is filled with animals from the rain forest. For other travelers who want to go farther upriver, this is the start of another journey. The most adventurous board a cargo boat and set off again toward the city of Iquitos in Peru.

The air is heavy with moisture, and the heat becomes difficult to bear. From time to time, sudden showers whip the deck, sending the passengers hurrying below for shelter. At night, the air is clear and cool and alive with the croaking of frogs, the shrieking of birds, and other sounds of the rain forest.

On smaller tributaries far away from the main river live groups of Amazonian people. For many of these people, life follows a simple pattern of hunting and gathering nuts and berries.

Past Manaus, the forest reaches down to the bank. Giant trees overhang the water, and their branches spread out to form a huge, green umbrella. Many kinds of flowering plants and vines reach upward for their share of light.

Here and there the boat stops to pick up or drop off passengers. The captain always looks for people waving from the bank. Some are carrying armfuls of vegetables, fruits, or chickens to be sold at towns farther upriver. Soon the boat is noisy and full of color.

In places, the trees have been cut down for their timber or to make way for villages set in small clearings. From the river, a few corrugated tin roofs mark the village huts, which are often set on stilts to raise them above the water. The people living here depend on the river for their contact with the outside world. The traders bring food, tools, and guns, which the people exchange for nuts, rubber, wood, or skins.

Woolly monkeys and sloths live in the safety of the thick rain forest. Flame-colored macaws and emerald-green hummingbirds decorate the trees. Below them, the jaguar stalks its prey.

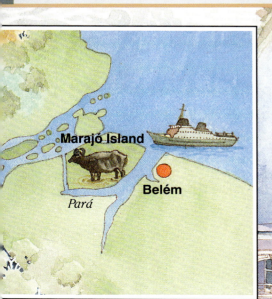

At last Iquitos is in sight. At one time this city was a busy town, important for its rubber. Many traders made fortunes. They built beautiful Portugese-style houses, decorated with balconies and with patterned tiles on the walls. The tourists wander through the lively streets, buying pottery, embroidery, and other crafts made by Indians. Visitors to Iquitos are always aware of the great, green rain forest close by. It is a fine place to explore at the end of a long journey.

Welcome to the cold lands

The cold lands are in the far north and far south of our planet. These frozen areas are called the Arctic in the north and the Antarctic in the south.

Antarctica is a continent in its own right. There is land in places in Antarctica, but most of it is hidden under hundreds of feet (meters) of ice. There are several scientific bases where people can live for short times, despite the cold and isolation.

There is no land at the North Pole—only sea and ice. The Arctic is a large, frozen ocean. Several countries lie partly inside the Arctic Circle. These include Canada, Norway, Sweden, and Russia.

Supply ships take food and fuel to the scientific bases in Antarctica.

Scientists from many countries work at research stations in Antarctica.

South Atlantic Ocean

Weddell Sea

ice

ice

ANTARCTICA

ice

Indian Ocean

+ **South Pole**

South Pacific Ocean

Southern Ocean

ice

Ross Sea

Antarctic Circle

266

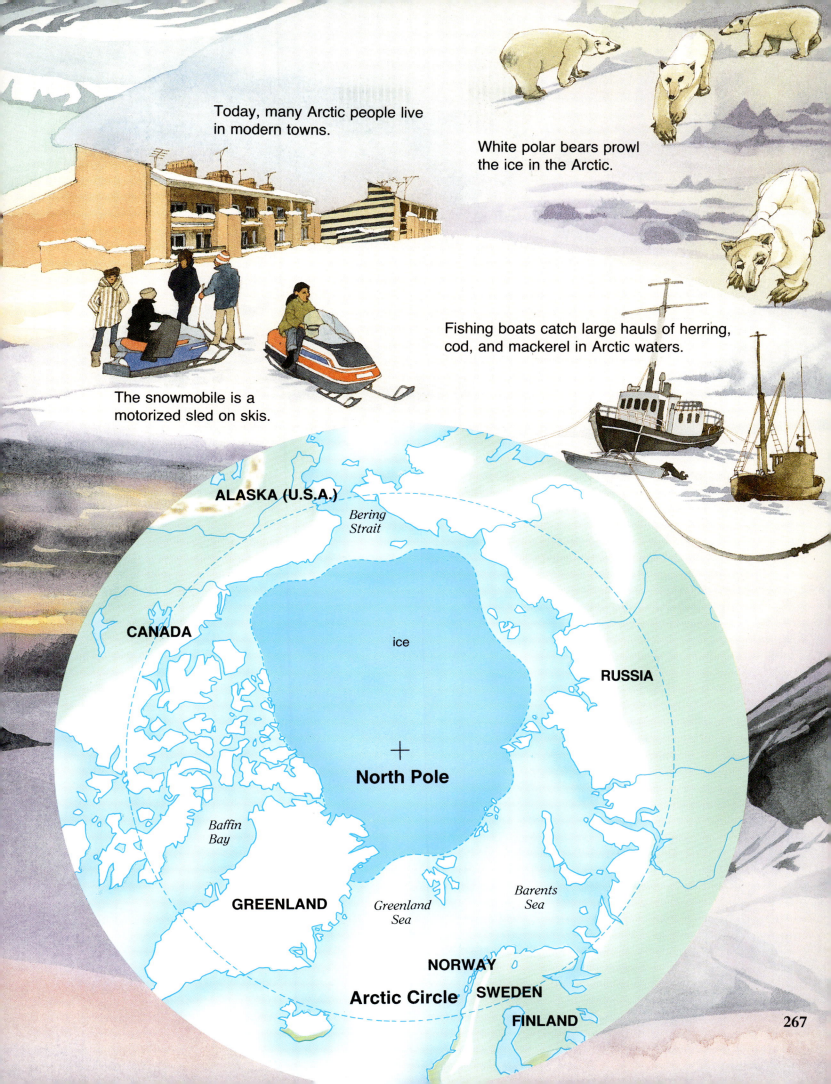

Today, many Arctic people live in modern towns.

White polar bears prowl the ice in the Arctic.

The snowmobile is a motorized sled on skis.

Fishing boats catch large hauls of herring, cod, and mackerel in Arctic waters.

ALASKA (U.S.A.)

Bering Strait

CANADA

ice

RUSSIA

+ North Pole

Baffin Bay

GREENLAND

Greenland Sea

Barents Sea

NORWAY

Arctic Circle

SWEDEN

FINLAND

Life in the Arctic

In winter, the Arctic is a cold, dark place. The days are short and the nights are very long. There is little sunshine. But in the summer months, between May and August, it is very different. At this time of year it is often warm and sunny. In places, the ground is covered with hundreds of different grasses and brightly colored flowers.

Huge herds of reindeer and caribou graze on the treeless plains, or tundra. There are also many small animals. Birds and mosquitos fill the air.

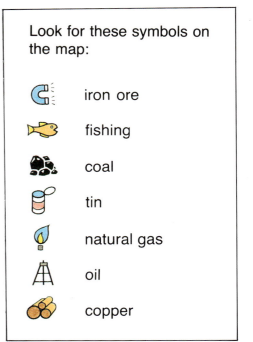

Look for these symbols on the map:

iron ore	
fishing	
coal	
tin	
natural gas	
oil	
copper	

The Arctic seas are full of fish that are caught in the summer by trawlers. Around the edges of the Arctic there is mining for coal and other minerals. Oil rigs are sometimes damaged by storms or floating blocks of ice.

polar bear

caribou

reindeer

arctic fox

ringed seal

skua

arctic poppy

lousewort

buttercup

walrus

tundra willow

268

The main people of the Arctic are the Inuit of Canada, the Yuit of Siberia, and the Sami of Norway, Sweden, and Finland. Those who follow traditional ways live by fishing and hunting. They wear padded clothes and thick shoes to keep warm.

Inuit children usually spend most of the year at school. But during the summer vacation, they learn to fish.

North Pole

269

Life in the Antarctic

Antarctica is empty and very bleak. People do not live in the Antarctic. They visit only to explore and study its land. Icy winds gust, often at gale force, catching the loose snow and blowing it about in swirling blizzards. Little can be heard except the howling of the wind. It is the coldest place on earth. All year, most of the land is buried under a thick layer of ice and snow. A small area is free of ice, and some mountain peaks rise above it.

Antarctica is the land surrounding the South Pole. Around it lies a cold sea made up of the Southern Ocean and the southernmost parts of three other oceans, the Indian, Pacific, and Atlantic.

Few plants can grow in Antarctica and those that do are very small. The ground is too cold for plants that need to grow long roots. Moss and lichen are found on ice-free patches of ground, but there are only a few kinds of plants that flower.

The seas around Antarctica are icy and stormy. Most of the sea freezes in winter. It forms pack ice. In summer, the pack ice begins to thaw and breaks up in large chunks.

Icebreakers smash the ice so that other ships can pass.

McMurdo Station, a research base on Ross Island, has Antarctica's largest community. About 1,000 people live there during the warmer months. Fewer live there in the winter.

Scientists from many nations study the wildlife, ice, and rocks. Below, an Adélie penguin watches as a scientist measures and marks its egg.

Life in the sea

The sea is home to thousands of birds and mammals. There are many types of seals and whales, which feed on the mixture of microscopic plants and fish that float in vast patches near the surface of the sea. Sea birds dive from great heights to catch fish, and penguins slip in from the ice for the same food. Whales, seals, and penguins have thick layers of fat, called blubber, under their skins to keep them warm.

King penguin

Adélie penguin

Emperor penguin

Ross seal

Weddell seal

crabeater seal

humpbacked whale

Blue whale

finbacked whale

leopard seal

South Pole

271

Looking at the land

Ships that enter the icy seas of the Antarctic make their way slowly and cautiously. Usually they are carrying food, fuel, and other supplies to scientists working in the region.

Around the coasts of Antarctica are high cliffs of ice. The cliffs are the edges of an ice shelf—a huge block of ice jutting out from the shore. In places, the ice on Antarctica is up to three miles (5 km) thick. Much of the world's snow and ice is piled up on Antarctica. Many high mountains are buried under the ice. Only the tops of the highest mountains jut out. On some parts of the coast, especially on the Antarctic Peninsula, the snow and ice melt in the summer. Parts of the ice break away from the land and form icebergs.

Spectacular volcanoes stand against the icy scenery of the Antarctic. Some volcanoes are still steaming. **Deception Island,** in the South Shetland Islands, has some active volcanoes.

Icebergs are huge chunks of floating ice that have broken off from glaciers. Only about one-eighth of the ice can be seen above the water. The rest floats under the sea. The largest iceberg ever seen came from Antarctica. It had an area larger than Belgium.

An ice shelf juts out over the **Ross Sea.** It is about the same size as the country of France. It is now the largest piece of floating ice in the world.

The **Weddell Sea** is a giant bay that cuts into the west coast of Antarctica. Almost half of the bay is always frozen over.

South
Atlantic
Ocean

Indian
Ocean

**Deception
Island**

Weddell
Sea

ice

ice

ice

South
Pacific
Ocean

+

South Pole

ice

Mount Erebus

Ross
Sea

Southern
Ocean

Mount Erebus is an active volcano. From time to time, it throws pieces of volcanic rock into the air.

Glossary

Antarctic The Antarctic is the area around the South Pole. It includes Antarctica, the name of the continent in this region, and the waters around it.

Arctic The Arctic is the name given to the large, cold area around the North Pole.

atoll An atoll is a ring of coral rock or a ring of islands around an area of shallow water.

bauxite Bauxite is an ore or mineral from which the metal aluminum is made.

broad-leaved Some trees, such as the maple and the walnut have broad, flat leaves. In temperate regions, many kinds of broad-leaved trees lose their leaves in autumn.

Buddhist A Buddhist is a follower of Buddhism, one of the main religions of the world.

cacao Cacao is an evergreen tree whose seeds, or beans, are used to make chocolate or cocoa.

cassava Cassava is a tropical plant that is an important source of food.

century A century is a period of one hundred years. The 15th century is the time between 1401 to the end of 1500. The 16th century is the time between 1501 and 1600. We are living in the 21st century.

Christian A Christian is a follower of Christianity, one of the main religions of the world.

climate The climate of a particular place is its weather over a long period of time.

cocoon A cocoon is a soft covering of silky threads that a caterpillar spins around itself before changing into an adult insect.

colony When one country is controlled by another, more powerful country, it is sometimes known as a colony.

Communism Communism is a way of governing a country in which all or most of the property is owned by the government and shared by the people.

conifer A conifer is a tree that bears cones. Most conifers, such as pines, firs, and cedars, are evergreen and have needles.

continent A continent is a very large area of land often surrounded by oceans and usually containing several countries.

copra Copra is the dried white flesh of the coconut.

coral Coral is a hard material formed by the skeletons of millions of small sea animals.

dam A dam is a barrier built across a river to hold back the water. A lake of water usually builds up behind the dam.

delta A delta is a low area of land at the mouth of a river. It is formed by sand, stones, and mud that have been carried downstream by the river.

democracy Democracy is a system of government in which those in power are elected by the people.

dependency A dependency is a country that is part of a larger country but is often free to make its own laws and run its own affairs.

deposit A deposit is a layer of material in the ground, such as mud or sand. Mineral deposits include iron and gold.

election An election is the choosing of people to represent others. Elections are held to choose governments.

equator The equator is an imaginary line that circles the earth, halfway between the North Pole and the South Pole.

evergreen An evergreen tree has green leaves or needles all year long.

export An export is something that is sent to another country to be sold.

fertile Fertile land is land in which plants grow well. It is good for crop growing.

fungi Fungi are spongy plants without flowers or leaves.

glacier A glacier is a large mass of ice that moves very slowly, usually down a mountain valley.

gorge A gorge is a narrow valley with steep, rocky sides.

274

government A government is a group of people who rule a country or a state.

grain Grain describes the seeds of cereal plants, such as wheat, rice, and corn.

habitat A habitat is the place where a wild plant or animal normally lives.

head of state The king, queen, or president of a country is often called its head of state.

herb An herb is a small plant, usually with a soft stem.

hibernation Hibernation describes a kind of deep sleep that helps some animals survive through the cold winter.

Hindu A Hindu is a follower of Hinduism, one of the main religions of the world.

immigrant An immigrant is someone who goes to live permanently in another country.

import An import is something that has been brought into a country from another country.

independence Independence means being free from the control of others. Countries that have obtained the right to govern themselves have gained their independence.

industry Industry is a general name for the whole process of making things. Industry is also the name for any particular type of business, such as the steel industry or the tourist industry.

irrigation Irrigation describes the way in which people bring water to dry land by canals or pipes so that crops will grow.

Islam Islam is the name of the Muslim religion, one of the main religions of the world.

Jew A Jew is a follower of Judaism, one of the main religions of the world.

lagoon A lagoon is a saltwater lake separated from the sea by a sandbank or a coral reef.

latex The white gum produced by the rubber tree is called latex.

livestock Livestock describes animals that are raised for food and other products, such as wool or leather.

manufacture To manufacture things is to make them, usually with machines.

monarchy A monarchy is a country where the head of state is a king or queen, emperor, or sultan.

monsoon A monsoon is a seasonal wind. Dry northeasterly winds blow across India in winter. In summer, monsoon winds blow from the southwest. They usually bring heavy rain.

mosque A mosque is a religious building where Muslims pray.

Muslim A Muslim is a follower of Islam, one of the main religions of the world.

natural resource Products that are found naturally or which grow in a country are its resources. Sunshine, a good water supply, and oil are kinds of natural resources.

nomad A nomad is a person who has no fixed home and who travels from place to place as a way of life.

oasis An oasis is a place in the desert where water rises to the surface, making the land more fertile.

ore Ore is a mineral or rock that contains enough of a metal to make it worth mining.

outback The outback is the area of dry grassland and desert in central Australia.

pampas The pampas is an area of grassy plains in South America.

parliament The parliament of a country is the group of people who make the laws.

plain A plain is a large, flat area of land.

plantation A plantation is a large area of land that has been planted with a single crop such as coffee, sugar cane, or trees.

plateau A plateau is a high, flat plain. Another word for plateau is tableland.

pollution Pollution is the act of dirtying or destroying the world around us. Pollution can harm the soil, the water, and the air.

population The population of a country or an area is the number of people who live there.

prairie The prairies are flat grasslands in North America.

republic A republic has a government elected by the people to rule the country, but no king or queen. The president is usually the head of state in a republic.

rift valley A rift valley is a valley made when the earth's crust moved, causing parts of the land to drop to a lower level.

savanna A savanna is a large area of grassy land with few trees, especially one in a warm region.

sea level The level of the ocean waters is known as sea level. Land is measured as a certain number of feet above or below sea level.

sediment Sediment is the sand or soil that is carried along by running water or a glacier.

stalactite A stalactite is a spike of rock that hangs from the roof of a cave.

stalagmite A stalagmite is a cone-shaped stump of rock that sticks up from the floor of a cave.

state A state is a country or a part of a country.

steel Steel is a very strong metal that is made from iron, carbon, and other minerals.

steppes The steppes are the huge grasslands of Russia. They are like the vast prairies of North America, but are much colder in the winter.

subcontinent A subcontinent is a large area of land that forms an important part of a main continent.

suburb A suburb is an area of housing on the edge of a town or city.

sultan Some Muslim countries are ruled by a sultan, who is a kind of king.

taiga The taiga is a vast area of forest that stretches across subarctic regions of Russia and Canada.

temperate Temperate describes the weather in a region where it is neither very hot nor very cold.

terrace Hillsides are sometimes cut in steps, or terraces. Crops can be grown on the flat terraces.

textiles Textiles is a general term for fabrics, cloth, carpets, and rugs.

thresh To thresh wheat or other cereal plants is to beat them in order to remove the grains.

timber Timber is wood that is used for building or carpentry.

tributary A tributary is a river or stream that flows into a larger river.

Tropic of Cancer The Tropic of Cancer is an imaginary line around the world that marks the northern extent of the tropics.

Tropic of Capricorn The Tropic of Capricorn is an imaginary line around the world that marks the southern extent of the tropics.

tropics The tropics is an area of the earth that lies between the Tropic of Cancer and the Tropic of Capricorn. It is hot all year around in the tropics.

tundra The tundra is a cold, dry region where trees cannot grow. Tundras are covered by snow more than half the year. In spring and summer, the snow melts and plants grow for part of the year.

tungsten Tungsten is a very strong metal and can stand great heat without melting. It is used in making the filaments for light bulbs.

valley A valley is a low-lying stretch of land between hills. Rivers often flow through valleys.

volcano A volcano is an opening in the earth's surface through which hot melted rock, ash, and gases are forced out. Volcanoes can be active, which means they continue to erupt, or inactive, which means that they have not erupted for a long time.

weather The weather describes how cold, hot, or wet a place is, and if there is sunshine, rain, snow, or wind.

Index

Index

Index

Index

Index

Resources: Where to find out more

For your globe-trotting pleasure, check out these books, software, videos, and Web sites.

Amazon Trail 3rd Edition: Rainforest Adventures, CD-ROM for Mac and Windows; The Learning Company, 2000.
Plan your journey up the Amazon River carefully. Hopefully, you'll avoid the piranhas and other dangers and get to know the Amazon people and their rain forest environment instead.

Around the World in Eighty Days, by Jules Verne; Puffin Classics, 2004.
Written in 1873, long before jet airplanes existed, this charming novel describes the 80-day journey of the English gentleman Phileas Fogg and his French servant Passepartout. Follow their adventures as they circle the globe by railroad, ship, sled, and even elephant, meeting many interesting characters along the way—all to win a bet!

Children from Australia to Zimbabwe, by Maya Ajmera and Anne Rhesa Versola; Charlesbridge, 2001.
How are kids around the world like you and different from you? This alphabet book about countries is full of interesting facts and beautiful photographs.

CIA's Homepage for Kids, http://www.cia.gov/cia/ciakids, by Central Intelligence Agency.
Ready for a CIA geography quiz? Even if you're not, this site has codes to try to break, virtual tours, and maps and facts about all the countries in the world.

Down in the Subway, by Miriam Cohen; Star Bright Books, 2003.
Oscar meets Island Lady one day on the New York subway. All she has to do is smile her fine Island smile, open her bag, and the whole train turns into a rollicking Caribbean experience.

Families of Israel, video, 29 minutes; Vide-O-Go/That's Infotainment 2000.
Israeli kids introduce you to their families and their lives in this excellent video. Other titles in the Families of the World series feature Brazil, China, Egypt, France, Ghana, India, Japan, Korea, Mexico, Puerto Rico, Russia, Sweden, Thailand, the United Kingdom, and the United States. Contact Families of the World at http://www.familiesoftheworld.com for online ordering information.

Faraway Home, by Jane Kurtz; Harcourt/Gulliver, 2000.
Desta's father tells her about his life growing up in Ethiopia as he gets ready to return to his homeland to care for his ailing mother. Beautiful illustrations help capture the contrast between an American and an Ethiopian childhood.

Jungle Islands, My South Sea Adventure, by Maria Coffey and Debora Pearson; Annick, 2000.
Are you ready for a kayaking trip through the Solomon Islands in the Pacific? Author Maria Coffey takes you along on her trip. Beautiful photographs help tell the story of the islands—their people, animals, natural wonders, and history.

Kids Around the World Celebrate!, by Lynda Jones; Wiley, 2000.
From Chinese New Year to a carnival in Venice, Italy, join the many celebrations of people all over the world, thirteen countries to be exact. Activities and recipes for special foods make the celebrations even more fun.

National Geographic.Com Kids, http://www.nationalgeographic.com/kids, by National Geographic.
Check out the creature features, geo challenges, jokes, mystery pictures, the GeoBee challenge, and many other activities at this awesome Web site. It's hard to run out of things to do here.

On the Same Day in March: A Tour of the World's Weather, by Marilyn Singer; HarperCollins, 2000.
The youngest readers will enjoy this picture-book journey to seventeen places in the world. My, how the weather varies from place to place!

Savage Earth Online, http://www.thirteen.org/savageearth, by PBS.
The animation and video on this excellent Web site about powerful earth forces give you a front-row seat to natural disasters, such as volcanoes, tsunamis, and earthquakes.

The Top of the World: Climbing Mount Everest, by Steve Jenkins; Houghton, 1999.
Find out all about Everest and the daring adventurers who have climbed it. The author has illustrated this beautiful book with amazing paper cut-out collages.

Where Is That?, http://www.funbrain.com/where/index.html, by The Learning Network.
One or two players can test their geography with this Internet map quiz game. You get to choose level of difficulty and the part of the world on which to quiz yourself.